NEXT HOUSE

Architecture for the Twenty-First Century

Ron Broadhurst

Abrams, New York

Editor
Aiah R. Wieder

Designer
Beatriz Cifuentes - Caballero

Production Manager
Alison Gervais

Cataloging-in-Publication Data has been applied for
and may be obtained from the Library of Congress.
ISBN 978-0-8109-5401-4

Printed and bound in China
10 9 8 7 6 5 4 3 2 1

Abrams books are available at special discounts
when purchased in quantity for premiums
and promotions as well as fundraising or
educational use. Special editions can also be
created to specification. For details, contact
specialmarkets@abramsbooks.com
or the address below.

ABRAMS
THE ART OF BOOKS SINCE 1949
115 West 18th Street
New York, NY 10011
www.abramsbooks.com

The close of the first decade of the twenty-first century seems a particularly rich period at which to consider the state of domestic architecture around the globe, and the process of compiling a survey of houses that somehow express the most relevant currents in house-building required the consideration of an array of factors, including geographic range, environmental sustainability, and—of course—formal boldness. Particularly fascinating was the degree to which the innovative architects featured in these pages look to the past, reconsidering the lessons of the masters of twentieth-century modernism, or facing the challenge of "remaking" forward-looking spaces in structures that are decades or even centuries old. But whether occupying an eighteenth-century London church tower or standing as an enigmatic tentlike structure in the Chilean highland, these houses represent the vanguard of domestic design at the turn of the millennium.

Any discussion of the state of the art of house-building during the early twenty-first century must begin with the revolution in house-building during the early and mid-twentieth century. By the 1920s, the leading lights of progressive design, particularly Mies van der Rohe and Le Corbusier, laid the foundations for an "International Style" of modernist architecture, which stripped away the ornamentation and eclecticism of traditional styles in favor of a new structural expressiveness and spatial fluidity.

The elder statesman among the architects whose work is featured in these pages, Tadao Ando has devoted his career to refining the principles of the International Style—among them simple, rectilinear forms with planar surfaces stripped of ornamentation—into a mature signature style compatible with the aesthetic and building traditions of his native Japan. This style, whether at the modest of scale of the 4 x 4 House (page 16) or that of the more expansive cultural commissions such as the Modern Art Museum of Fort Worth and numerous museums in Japan, is dependent upon the precise execution of his austere structures, almost invariably in perfectly cast concrete. Similarly, the work of Spanish architect Alberto Campo Baeza emerges from a purist approach to material and form, beginning with a series of pristine white stucco houses in Spain and evolving to embrace expanses of concrete and glass, as in the Olnick

Spanu House (page 218), the glazed upper story of which is an exemplary essay in Miesian attenuation and transparency.

The quality that has allowed classical modernism to endure with such vitality into this century is its nearly infinite adaptability—a quality demonstrated by Marcio Kogan's Casa BR outside of Rio de Janeiro (page 34), and Pezo von Ellrichshausen Architects' Casa Poli on the remote Chilean seacoast (page 80). And the exhilarating cascade of building forms that compose Casa Tóló (page 44)—designed by Álvaro Leite Siza Vieira, son of the great Portuguese architect Álvaro Siza—attests to the durability of modernist principles not only across borders but across generations.

A more primitivist, less obviously refined strand of modernism emerges in Fearon Hay Architects' Mountain Retreat (page 212), with a basic formal profile that recalls Le Corbusier's Petite Maison de Weekend—built of stone, concrete, and a turf roof—but with a warm and opulent interior more evocative of a weekend getaway as envisioned by Tom Ford. The Presenhuber House (page 188), designed by Andreas Fuhrimann and Gabrielle Hächler—who recast the traditional architecture of Switzerland's Engadine Valley in concrete and plywood—is also informed by the spirit of Le Corbusier, whose earliest commissions in his native alpine town of La Chaux-de-Fonds emulated the chalets found throughout the region. An unconventional site provided the inspiration for Caruso St. John Architects' catacomblike series of rooms composing the Brick House (page 56), organized within the residual space at the ends of three rows of London terrace houses; but even here the faintest whisper of Le Corbusier can be detected in the contemplative interior spaces, not only in their rough yet elegant concrete and brick surfaces, but also in the ceilings punctuated by numinous apertures that recall the overhead oculi illuminating the chapel of the monastery at La Tourette. An even more primal spirit generated Sou Fujimoto's meandering House O (page 180), which extends in desultory fashion along its coastline site like an anemone washed in from the Pacific Ocean. Here Fujimoto's point of reference is not the work of the "primitive" modernist master Le Corbusier but an edenic vision of architecture as landscape form, with the house's plan conceived as a trail leading from room to room.

Like Fujimoto's House O, Steven Holl's Turbulence House (page 62) derives its form from a natural metaphor—in this case, the tip of an iceberg. But what truly distinguishes this project is the experimental character of its design and construction. In order to realize his design for the 900-square-foot guest house—aided by digital three-dimensional modeling software—Holl turned to A. Zahner and Co., a Kansas City–based sheet metal manufacturing company whose high level of craftsmanship, combined with skillful digital formal manipulation, has been honed over the course of collaborations with Frank Gehry on much larger-scale projects, such as the Guggenheim Museum Bilbao and the Walt Disney Concert Hall in Los Angeles. Digital engineering technology also played a major role in the design and construction of Kraus Schönberg Architects' Haus W (page 200), though here the scope of experimentation was much more modest and practical: prefabricated, digitally cut and processed timber panels compose the walls and floors of the house's upper floor and represent the successful application of recyclable materials and a cost-effective system of construction in the service of an innovative design.

Where the great experimenters of the last century were stripping away ornamentation and creating free-flowing spaces, today's experimenters are pioneering research into the potential of new materials for both formal invention and environmental sustainability. In the case of the striking Wall House (page 168), designed by Chilean firm FAR frohn&rojas, bold design and innovative materials are inextricable. Composed of four sets of concentric wall systems, the Wall House utilizes unconventional materials—high-insulation polycarbonate panels and a synthetic fabric membrane—for two of these wall systems, which operate in concert to maximize insulation and minimize solar heat gain. Other energy-conserving strategies implemented in the Wall House include a gas-powered radiant heating system in the ground floor plane and a passive cooling system composed of PEX tubing.

Perhaps most dedicated to the ideal of sustainability among the architects whose work is featured in this volume are Werner Sobek, in Germany, and Sean Godsell, in Australia. Sobek's H16 (page 132) is certainly the most ecologically ambitious of these projects, claiming a structural system composed entirely of recyclable materials and a host of strategies—including geothermal heating and photovoltaic panels—that not only minimize energy consumption but actually produce a surplus of energy. Godsell's austere and elegant St. Andrews Beach House (page 96) may achieve a less spectacular degree of energy conservation than the singular H16, but the otherworldly structure is one in an impressive line of essays in sustainability undertaken since Godsell established his own practice in 1994.

As with all of his projects, Godsell looked back to the traditional vernacular structures of the Australian outback to create a formally forward-looking house that relies on simple yet effective methods of passive energy conservation. For their Beach House (page 114), Peter Stutchbury and Phoebe Pape, also based in Australia, relied on Pape's experience as a landscape designer to open the house to a range of landscape and water elements, keeping the house cool as well as virtually dissolving any transition between interior and exterior. A longer view of sustainability informed Yung Ho Chang's approach to designing the Split House (page 10), in China. Like Godsell, Chang looked to the past to realize his vision for a prototype structure that would have the absolute minimal impact on its site. Here the precedent was traditional earth-and-wood construction, which ensures that the house will disintegrate completely if simply left alone for a long enough period of time.

Chang is not the only architect featured in these pages whose ambitions extend beyond a single dwelling to the development of a replicable prototype, though his cohort, Winy Maas of the Dutch firm MVRDV, could not have embarked on his prototypical experiment in a context more different than the mountainous region north of Beijing. Didden Village (page 152), which rests atop a loft building in downtown Rotterdam, not only embodies Maas's vision for the rejuvenation of rooftops in any number of urban centers but also represents a delightful example of adaptive reuse, incorporating as it does the existing top floor of a former warehouse. Like the Didden Village loft project, David Chipperfield Architects' House in Manhattan (page 26) occupies a conventional venue for the reuse of an existing structure, in this case a nineteenth-century town house. However, the architects' intervention is anything but conventional, most notably for the introduction of a sculptural oak staircase that winds in dramatic fashion through the house's five stories.

Without a doubt the most ambitious example of adaptive reuse in this volume is Boyarsky Murphy Architects' Christ Church Tower (page 142), where all the spaces that would comprise an otherwise sprawling bourgeois residence are nestled over twelve levels of nooks, mezzanines, and vaults. Messana O'Rorke Architects' revitalization of a much altered cottage dating from the eighteenth century effectively comprised two projects in one: The creation of Ten Broeck Cottage (page 72) involved both the sensitive yet bold reconstruction of the original structure and the design of an entirely new structure. For this new construction the architects chose to complement the existing cottage with an addition that would have a vocabulary all its own rather than refer to any traditional model. The result is a startling yet appealing COR-TEN steel–clad object that seems no more incompatible with its context than a similarly rough-edged sculpture.

The most startling and sculptural of all the projects featured here is likely UNStudio's VilLA NM (page 122), which enigmatically occupies its bucolic site like the perfect hybrid between suburban tract house and alien spacecraft. David Adjaye's Sunken House (page 160) maintains a similarly alien quality, though it has touched down in the middle of an East London neighborhood, politely interrupting the stolid rhythm of tidy rows of semidetached houses. Like the Sunken House, Assadi + Pulido's Deck House (page 106) is clad in dark-stained wood, putting a time-tested material into the service of a high-concept design that wraps its program within a single planar structure that unfurls down a spectacular site in the foothills of the Andes Mountains in Chile. Tezuka Architects' Atelier in Ushimado (page 230) is also clad in dark wood, though here the use of charred cedar, a traditional building material in the region, assumes special local significance. More distinctive than its wood cladding are the Atelier's serene, exquisitely composed interior spaces, which are the result of an especially sensitive collaboration between the architects and their art collector client. An exceptional client also made possible Eldridge Smerin's House in Highgate Cemetery (page 240), in this instance by giving the architects a free hand at coming up with a solution to an intriguing challenge: How to build a house with significant presence on a sliver of a site at the perimeter of a famed London cemetery? The architects found the answer in transparency, embracing the gothic prospect as if the surrounding necropolis were the most delightful cityscape their client could hope to survey from his concrete-and-glass aerie. And at the end of a long decade, such a contemplative view does not seem inappropriate. Rather it suggests the degree to which an ambitiously conceived, artfully realized house can embrace the starkest realities and offer some measure of quiet and ease to those inhabiting its spaces.

Yung Ho Chang, who has divided his time between projects in Beijing and teaching posts at the Massachusetts Institute of Technology and Harvard University's Graduate School of Design, sought to create with his Split House a structure that would have the absolute minimum impact on its surrounding natural context and that could be easily replicated. The first goal was achieved by following the time-honored local earth-and-wood construction method known as *tu mu*, which results in a structure that will disintegrate on its own once it is no longer in use. Here the construction is earthen walls compressed within laminated wood frames, providing excellent insulation and increased energy performance.

To create a prototype structure that could be implemented on sites throughout the hills north of Beijing, Chang turned to the capital's traditional urban courtyard houses for formal inspiration. There he found a building type that could be updated in modular fashion, offering flexibility for the arrangement of interior space as well as the configuration of multiple modules. In the Split House prototype, two modules were arranged to preserve certain trees on the site and to separate public and private spaces. Later construction could accommodate different configurations of these modules—set at right angles, stacked, arranged in parallel—depending on the requirements of the site. Here the public wing consists of a mah-jongg parlor and formal indoor and outdoor reception spaces, while the private wing comprises the family's kitchen, bedrooms, and informal living space, with both wings joined by a glass-enclosed foyer that features a natural stream running beneath its transparent glazed floor.

First floor

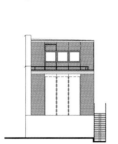

public wing

private wing

Second floor

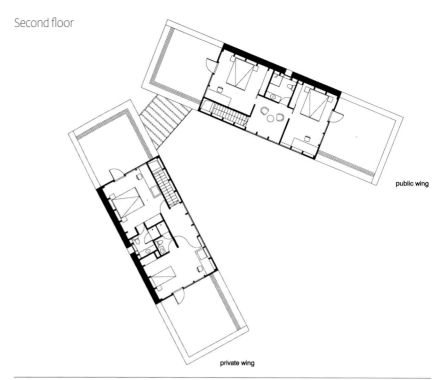

public wing

private wing

Northwest elevation, public wing

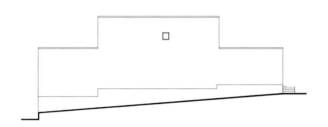

Southwest elevation, public wing

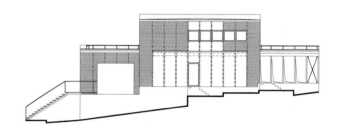

Southwest elevation, private wing

Southeast elevation, private wing

0	10	20 ft

Architect Yung Ho Chang conceived the
Split House as a prototype for modular dwellings
that could be replicated on sites throughout the
spectacular hills north of Beijing.

Above: By following the time-honored local earth-and-wood construction method known as *tu mu*, Yung Ho Chang developed a structure that will disintegrate on its own once it is no longer in use.

Opposite: The Split House's earthen walls compressed within laminated wood frames provide excellent insulation and increased energy performance.

The brief for the 4 x 4 House in Kobe, Japan, presented both a unique challenge and a unique inspiration to Tadao Ando, who for over three decades has created masterful compositions of concrete construction in Japan and abroad, including the Modern Art Museum of Fort Worth, Texas. Sited on a narrow sliver between the Inland Sea, which connects the Pacific Ocean to the Sea of Japan, and a heavily trafficked roadway, the 4 x 4 House by necessity required an almost shockingly small footprint: Only 16 square meters (172 square feet) of land were available for construction according to local code. Ando's approach to the site was also deeply informed by its proximity to Awaji Island, the epicenter of the Great Hanshin Earthquake of 1995. The result was a sentinel-like tower, rising high enough to provide living spaces arrayed on four levels, with views out to the island from the top.

Described by Ando as a "mimimum residence," the tower became for the architect an exploration of the limits of creating well-designed living spaces within extreme spatial constraints. At the ground level are entry and utility spaces, the second level contains a bedroom, the third level is a study, and kitchen and living space occupy the fourth level. This top level is distinguished by a double-height ceiling and a 1-meter (3-foot) extension out toward the sea to provide optimal views.

After the completion of the 4 x 4 House, Ando was approached by a potential client hoping to build another 4 x 4 House for himself. Ando not only accepted the commission, but recommended building the second house immediately adjacent to the first. This time, however, the house would be executed in wood, the material preferred by the new client. Now the lone sentinel is paired to become a sort of gateway, giving the two tiny houses a monumental dimension that fits nicely with Ando's original inspiration to let his 4 x 4 House commemorate a civic catastrophe that will be long remembered.

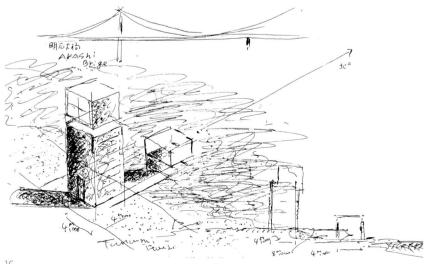

East elevation

North elevation

West elevation

South elevation

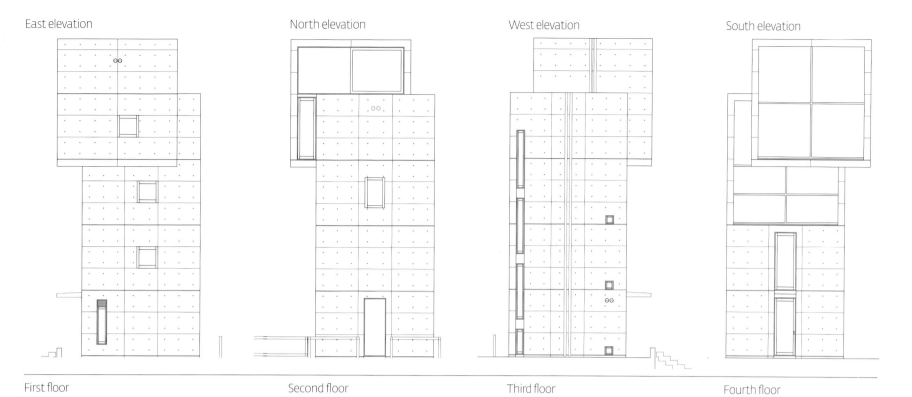

First floor

Second floor

Third floor

Fourth floor

 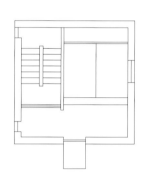 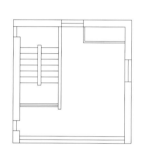 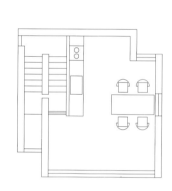

0   10 ft

0   2   5 m

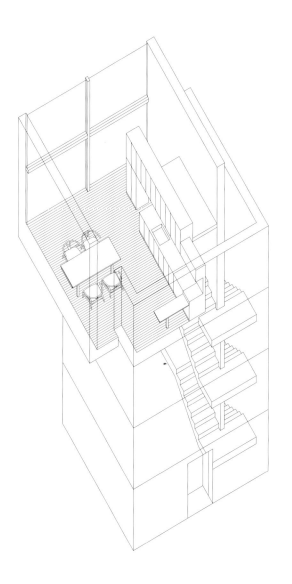

Opposite: The 4 x 4 House rises like a sentinel to provide living spaces arrayed on four levels, with views out to the Inland Sea from the top.

Above: The house is sited on a narrow sliver between the Inland Sea, which connects the Pacific Ocean to the Sea of Japan, and a heavily trafficked roadway, requiring a footprint of only 16 square meters (172 square feet).

Axonometric

The double-height kitchen/living space at the top of the tower offers expansive views of Japan's Inland Sea and demonstrates architect Tadao Ando's skill at creating well-designed living spaces within extreme spatial constraints.

Often lauded in the press as the best U.K.-based firm overlooked in its home country, David Chipperfield Architects has earned a solid international reputation on the merit of such projects as the Scottish headquarters for the BBC in Glasgow, the Figge Art Museum in Iowa, and the German Museum of Literature in Marbach. With the commission to renovate a five-story town house for a jet-setting bachelor, the firm once again found itself on foreign shores, this time in Manhattan's fashionable West Village, where it created a paradoxical study in discretion and flamboyance, in keeping with its consistently spectacular brand of minimalism.

On its face, the nineteenth-century house appears untouched, or perhaps the subject of a meticulously researched reconstruction job. The sober facade, so deferential to the rows of respectable houses that compose its picturesque neighborhood, gives away nothing of the radical intervention undertaken inside. With an original brief to transform the house's rambling interior into an open, kitchenless, thoroughly twenty-first-century one-bedroom dwelling—only slightly modified to include a minuscule guest bedroom and utilitarian caterer's kitchen—the architects were free to all but eliminate conventional partitions and doors, and to introduce a tour-de-force staircase that winds through the house like a pale oaken ribbon, uniting the free-flowing spaces into what Chipperfield calls a "vertical loft."

Here the warren of rooms originally created to serve a large nineteeth-century family have been combined into a few large, bright, and formally understated spaces: drawing room and dining room, library and master bedroom, and guest bedroom (really little more than an enclosed alcove proportioned like the most efficient ship's cabin), with a kitchen in the basement and a sleek, luxurious deck on the roof. An austere palette of materials and an extensive system of cabinets concealed by lacquered panels give pride of place to the dazzling sculptural staircase, as well as those most precious features of city living: abundant natural light and views.

Basement

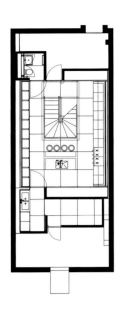

First floor

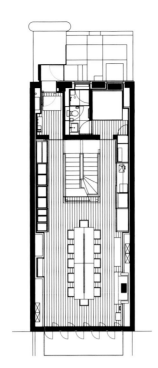

Second floor

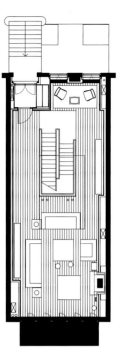

Third floor

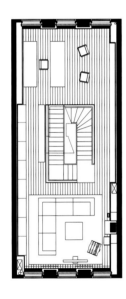

Fourth floor

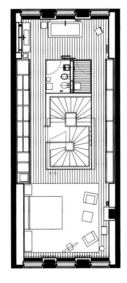

Roof

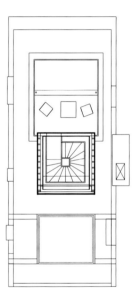

I   I   I
0   10   20 ft

Opposite: David Chipperfield Architects introduced a winding oak staircase into a nineteenth-century townhouse, creating a "vertical loft."

Right: Floor-to-ceiling glazing on the first two floors of the house's rear facade hint at the dramatic transformation of the interior spaces.

Sections

Inside the five-story house, a warren
of small, dark rooms was transformed into
a few large, bright, and formally
understated spaces with an austere palette
of materials and an extensive system of
cabinets concealed by lacquered panels.

Brazilian architect Marcio Kogan, who has an impressive portfolio of designs for luxury villas imbued with the spirit of Oscar Niemeyer's tropical-classical modernism, faced more than one remarkable constraint with this commission for a large house outside of Rio de Janeiro. First, the site, in the lush mountain region just north of Rio, presented a virtually Amazonian landscape with which to contend. Second, Kogan's brief included the incorporation of work started by another architect, who had been dismissed from the project. Out of these challenges Kogan crafted an exquisitely detailed modernist box that floats over its site like a sleek, luxurious tree house.

With a steel entrance bridge reaching from a hillside across a creek and a steel frame already constructed, the existing structure immediately suggested an organization favoring elevated living spaces. Kogan created a second-floor entrance platform as the terminus for the existing bridge, which leads to the open-plan, glass-enclosed main living space. Four large bedrooms comprise the house's more private zone: Where generous expanses of glass characterize the public living space, the sleeping spaces are notable for the heavy masonry walls enclosing even their outdoor terraces, which function as extremely secluded niches.

Kogan left the house's lower floor to function as a sort of grotto with an indoor swimming pool that can be opened to the surrounding rain forest via a system of completely retractable glass panels. Also contained on the ground level are a mechanical room, a sauna, and bathing facilities. Kogan clad the existing steel pillars in rich wood,which—together with the swimming area's ample exposed stonework—roots the jewel-like villa to its Edenic site.

Main floor

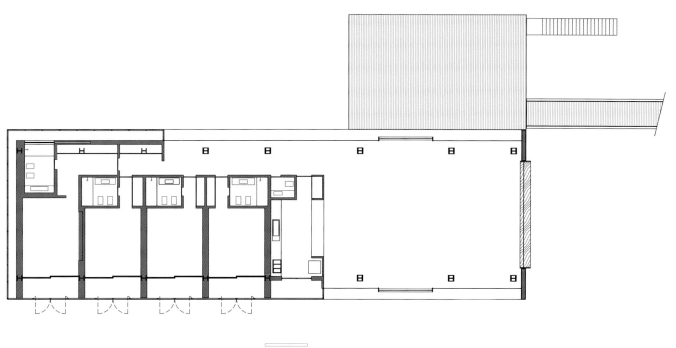

Lower floor

0   30 ft

Above: Architect Marcio Kogan conceived
Casa BR as an exquisitely detailed modernist
box that floats over its site like a sleek,
luxurious treehouse.

Opposite: A second-floor entrance platform
leads directly into the glass-enclosed open-plan
living room.

In the main living space, Kogan reduced
the visual barriers between the interior
space and the Amazonian landscape to
an absolute minimum.

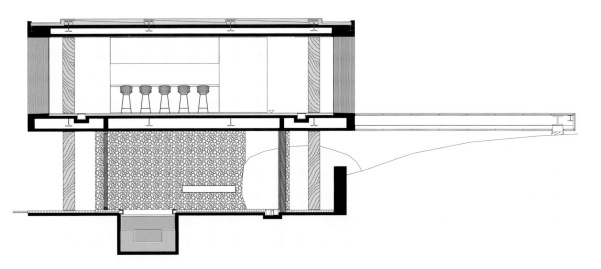

Opposite: The house's lower floor functions as a grotto with an indoor swimming pool that can be opened to the surrounding rain forest via a system of completely retractable glass panels.

Above: Kogan clad steel pillars in rich wood, reflecting the house's Edenic site throughout its interior spaces.

Section

Casa Tóló is an ingenious solution to an extreme topographical challenge—a series of concrete boxes that seem to tumble down a steep hillside. That the designer to arrive at this solution is the son of Pritzker Prize–winning master architect Álvaro Siza may have more than a little to do with the sophisticated and restrained realization of this spectacular concept. From the very start of the project's dramatic entry sequence, Siza produces the maximum effect with the minimum of formal gestures: At the top of the hillside site, one approaches an enigmatic platform that serves as a parking deck and hosts a gangway-style concealed stairway that descends more than two full flights to an entry landing and an office. The starkly linear staircase continues down to the main living level with the kitchen and on to the first of three bedroom modules, before fragmenting and shifting course in deference to the site's complicated topography.

Siza takes full advantage of the extraordinary sectional organization of the house to create myriad opportunities for formal playfulness in the spirit of one of his youthful influences, Piranesi: The roofs of the interior staircases serve as a series of exterior staircases that lead from the entry platform down the length of the house to a swimming pool at the structure's termination point. Inside, the stairs culminate in a jumble of pivoting half-flights of varying widths; partial views from inside to outside and from interior spaces up or down to other interior spaces create a complex sequence of clerestories. All of this is executed in exposed concrete, giving the otherwise ambitious project a monumental quality that makes it seem the inevitable result of its situation.

Floor plan and longitudinal section

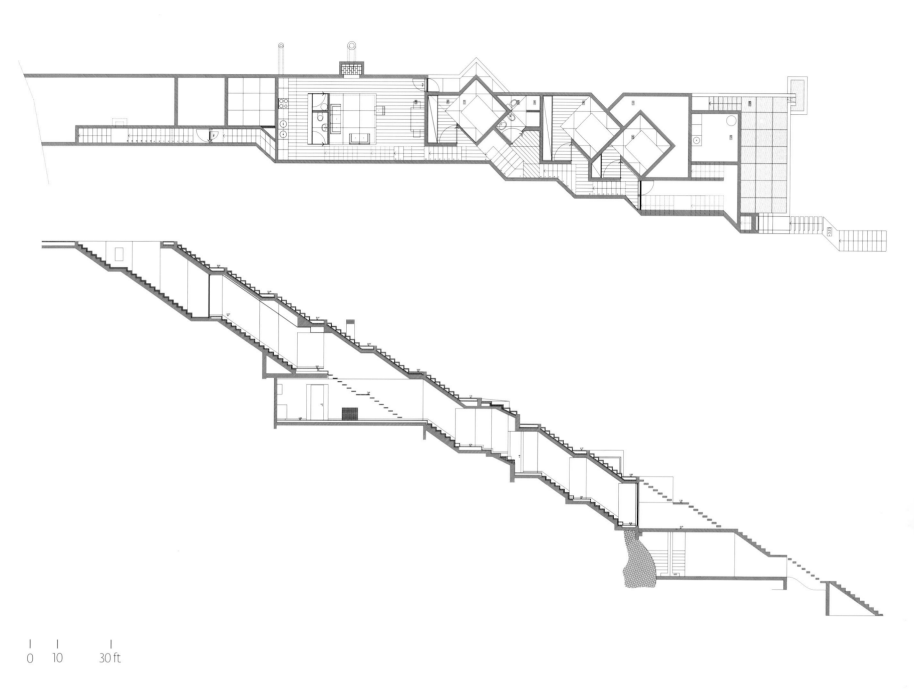

0   10   30 ft

Faced with the extreme topography of
Casa Tóló's spectacular site, architect
Álvaro Leite Siza Vieira created a series
of concrete boxes that seem to tumble
down a steep hillside.

The roofs of the house's interior staircases
serve as a series of exterior staircases
that lead down the length of the house
to a swimming pool at the structure's
termination point.

Opposite: Inside, the stairs culminate
in a jumble of pivoting half-flights of
varying widths.

Above: Partial views from inside to outside
and between interior spaces up or down
create a complex sequence of overlooks
and clerestories.

How do you build a habitable dwelling when your client presents you with an almost absurdly unbuildable site? Such was the challenge posed to London-based architects Adam Caruso and Peter St. John (known for their gallery and museum work, including the Gagosian Gallery's London outpost and the soon-to-be-completed Nottingham Centre for Contemporary Art) by a family determined to cobble together a living space out of a series of nooks and crannies hidden between three Victorian terrace houses. As is so often the case in twenty-first-century urban real estate markets, location trumped all spatial logic, though in this case the adventurous family had the wisdom to turn to architects who would arrive at an ingenious solution for making the impossible, horse head–shaped site into a sequence of unexpected yet meditative and calm spaces.

Because the new construction occupies nearly the entirety of the residual space between the surrounding buildings, its exterior form is elusive, only visible in tantalizing glimpses. Even the house's entrance is a bit of architectural sleight of hand, accessed behind an enigmatic door opening from the street to a long corridor that was once the driveway for its Victorian neighbor. The architects have compared the structure to an Italian Baroque chapel whose rich, solemn interior spaces are hidden deep within the engulfing fabric of the city.

The architects found their opportunity for formal and structural expression on the house's interior, which they conceived as a continuous membrane poured into the erratically shaped site and fashioned out of brick, a material that connotes structural stability and formal sobriety while simultaneously taking on an intricate fish scale–like quality as it undulates and contorts itself in various configurations within the mortar.
The upper-floor ceiling is fashioned out of cast concrete arranged at varying heights so that a low flat roof hangs over the dining table, for instance, while a steep dome soars over the main living space, creating a complex rhythm of compression and expansion once again evocative of the Baroque.

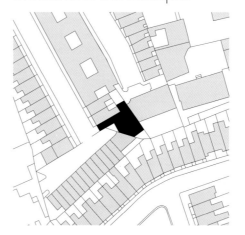

Lower level

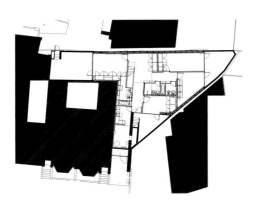

Upper level

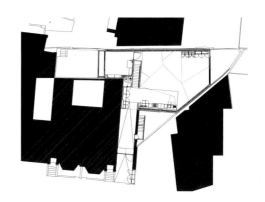

Sections

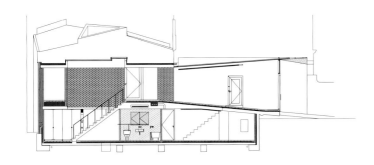

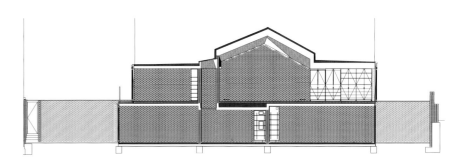

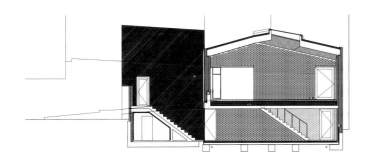

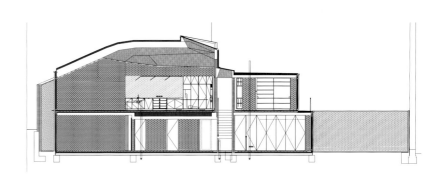

I   I   I
0   10   20 ft

Architects Caruso St. John fashioned the
Brick House out of a series of nooks and crannies
hidden between three Victorian terrace houses,
creating a complex yet serene sequence of
unexpected spaces.

Opposite: Walls are constructed
of traditional brick in a variety of
configurations, while ceilings are cast
concrete arranged at varying heights
and punctuated by expressively shaped,
vaulted skylights.

Above: Because of the house's unusual
site, the rare views out and external spaces
maintain a hermetic quality.

Steven Holl is an architect unafraid of metaphor. Indeed, his designs for a dormitory at the Massachusetts Institute of Technology (a study in porosity inspired by sponges), the Nelson-Atkins Museum of Art in Kansas City (conceived as a luminous series of lenses), and the soon-to-be-completed Linked Hybrid mixed-use complex in Beijing (intended as a "filmic city within a city") have earned Holl a reputation as the most poetic of early twenty-first-century modernists. Turbulence House, sited on a secluded, windswept mesa in the wilds of New Mexico, is just as rooted in metaphor as Holl's larger-scale projects. Here, this 900-square-foot guesthouse, commissioned by artist Richard Tuttle and poet Mei Mei Berssenbrugge, was born from the image of an iceberg's peak, intimating unseen depths.

In order to realize his highly poetic concept, Holl had to rely on advanced technology and adventurous craftsmen. The intricate, simultaneously faceted and curving facade was designed with the aid of digital three-dimensional modeling software, with the resulting forms executed by the same sheet metal manufacturers that have worked with Frank Gehry on such projects as the Guggenheim Museum Bilbao and the Walt Disney Concert Hall. With a sculptural breezeway creating an irregular arch, the finished exterior form of the house evokes not only the iceberg but also the dramatic topography of the surrounding desert canyon landscape.

The breezeway also allows the desert wind to move through the structure, providing passive cooling, one of several strategies to optimize energy performance. Other green strategies include the placement of photovoltaic panels on the house's south-facing roof, the use of a cistern to collect storm water from the roof for irrigation, and windows judiciously placed to reduce heat gain, quite small relative to the house's overall surface area, adding a level of experimental energy conservation to the formal invention in this rough jewel of a building.

First floor

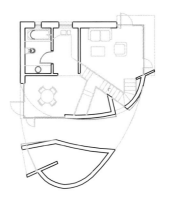

Second floor

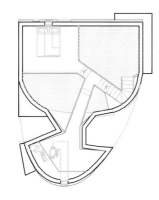

Roof

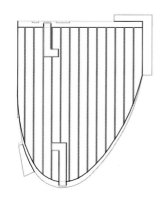

Southeast elevation

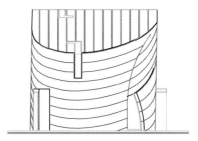

Southwest elevation

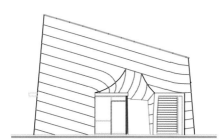

Northwest elevation

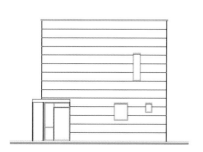

Northeast elevation

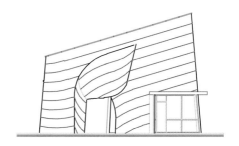

Cross section

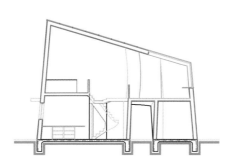

Cross section

| | |
0   6 ft

To realize the intricate facade of Turbulence House, architect Steven Holl turned to the same digital three-dimensional modeling software and sheet metal manufacturers employed for Frank Gehry's Guggenheim Museum Bilbao and the Walt Disney Concert Hall.

Above: Stairs lead from the compact living and dining/kitchen spaces to a sleeping loft and study.

Opposite: The main living space enjoys expansive views of the house's remote site on a New Mexico mesa.

The metal staircase to the eavelike upper floor leads to a bridge, also metal, that connects to a sleeping loft over the kitchen and bathroom, and a study, occupying a niche within the irregular arch that forms a breezeway on the house's exterior.

For this weekend house outside of New York City, architects Brian Messana and Toby O'Rorke effectively rewrote history with a vocabulary combining centuries-old wood and ultramodern weathering steel. The clients commissioned Messana and O'Rorke to renovate the interior of a small house dating back to 1734, while incorporating an entirely new structure to provide ample guest accommodations. While the original Dutch settlers' house was barely discernible in the much-renovated cottage, the clean lines and utilitarian spirit of early colonial construction inspired the architects' approach to both the cottage renovation and the design of the new structure.

Though it was impossible to determine the exact original appearance of the cottage, the architects extrapolated an exterior form consistent with eighteenth-century construction, starting with a fenestration system that used the oldest surviving window as a template; together with wide-board cedar siding and cedar roofing, these elements composed a classic American house form almost childlike in its directness and simplicity.

The interior of the cottage was assigned to contain the living room and dining room, separated by an elegant plaster through-wall fireplace, on the first floor, and two guest bedrooms with a shared bathroom tucked into the eaves of the second floor. Wide floorboards and rough-hewn ceiling beams on the ground level offer a warm contrast to the precisely executed plasterwork of the new walls.

For the addition, which contains kitchen, master bedroom, and cellar-level exercise room and sauna, the architects turned to an unlikely contemporary housing type for inspiration: the humble, even reviled trailer home. Separated from the original cottage by a glass-enclosed threshold, the addition occupies a simple rectilinear volume clad in COR-TEN steel, which will rust to take on an industrial appearance, complementing the warm tone of the cottage's cedar siding. Inside, limestone flooring sharply distinguishes itself from the antique floorboards inside the original cottage even as it matches their aesthetic clarity, while outside the two simple built forms—Dutch colonial cottage and steel-clad shed—express themselves with unexpected harmony.

Basement 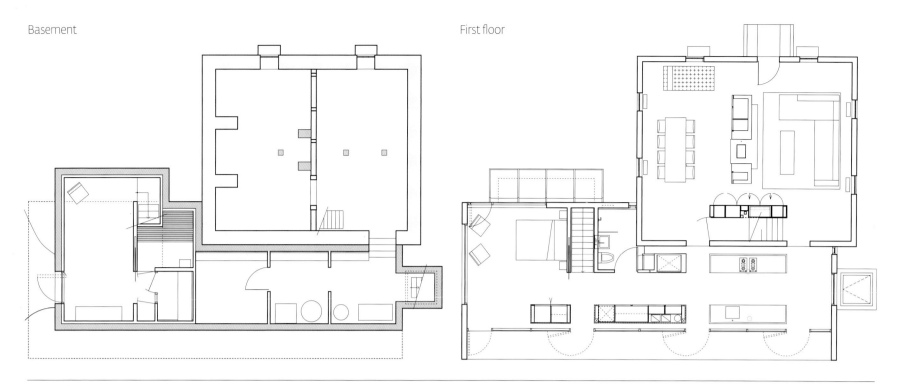   First floor

Second floor

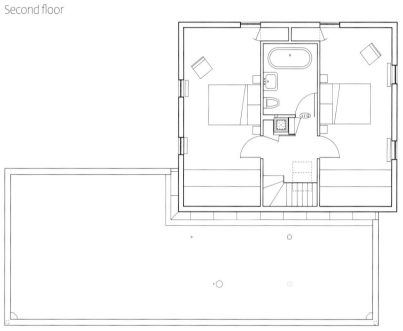

| | | |
| 0 | 3 | 12 ft |

Opposite: Messana O'Rorke Architects combined a wooden house from 1734 with an ultramodern steel addition to create Ten Broeck Cottage.

Above: Rough-hewn floorboards and ceiling beams in the original structure complement the sleek yet warm details of the new construction.

Above and opposite, top: The ground floor of the original structure contains the living room and dining room, separated by a new through-wall fireplace.

Opposite, bottom: Adjacent to the living and dining rooms is the kitchen, which occupies the new addition's main floor.

Opposite: The addition's cellar level contains a spare exercise room and sauna.

Above: Two guest bedrooms are tucked into the eaves of the original structure's upper level, while the master bedroom occupies the rear zone of the new addition.

Casa Poli Concepción, Chile Pezo von Ellrichshausen Architects 2005

Located on the Coliumo Peninsula, a rural setting sparsely populated by farmers, fishermen, and the occasional summer tourist, Casa Poli was conceived as a compact and autonomous volume crowning its sublime clifftop site as if it were a natural podium. The program required that the building function as both a summerhouse and a small art gallery and performance space. Therefore the interior had to mediate between maintaining one highly public aspect and another that was intimate and informal, with a scale that would be both monumental and domestic.

Such a multivalent program led the architects to create a series of interior spaces whose functions would remain indeterminate and flexible. To maximize this flexibility, all service elements—including kitchen, bathrooms, stairways, and closets—have been located within deep walls along the project's perimeter. These perimeter volumes also house interior balconies that can serve as storage space for all domestic accoutrements, completely freeing the main interior spaces for social and cultural functions.

A simple material palette of handmade concrete formed with untreated, battered wooden frames gives the building's modernist profile a richly primitive and highly tactile quality. The wooden frames used for the concrete formwork were also later made into interior door and window frames and sliding panels that conceal the various perimeter service elements and contribute even more to the house's primitivist/modernist character.

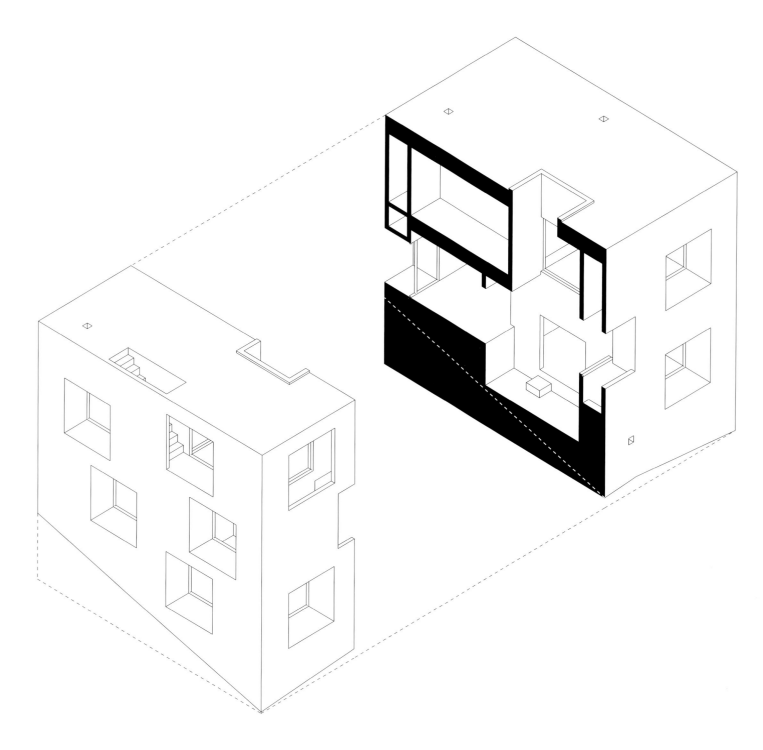

0	10	20 ft

Isometric section

First floor

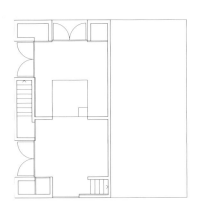

Second floor

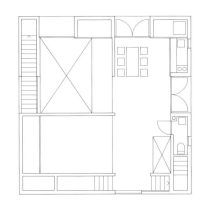

Third floor

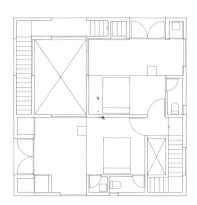

Terrace

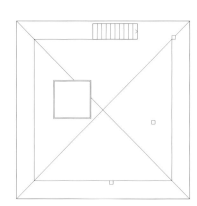

North elevation

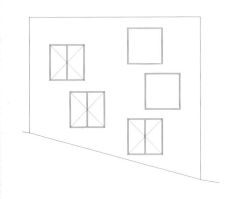

West elevation

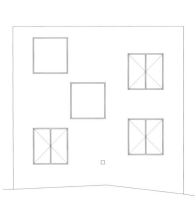

South elevation

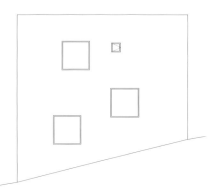

East elevation

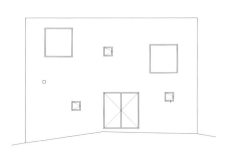

I   I   I
0   3   12 ft

Opposite: Voids and niches at the house's perimeter contain balconies, staircases, and corridors.

Right: The house's program called for a small gallery and performance space as well as a summer house, requiring Pezo von Ellrichshausen Architects to design a series of spaces that would be indeterminate and flexible.

Section

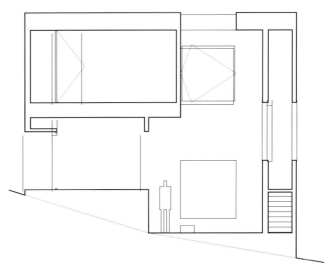

Above: Interior spaces flow openly into one another and around a central atrium space.

Opposite: In addition to circulation, the perimeter volumes also contain services such as the kitchen that can be concealed by sliding wooden panels.

Irregularly placed apertures punctuate
the house's overall cubic volume to provide
a variety of views and light conditions.

A simple material palette of handmade concrete
formed with untreated, battered wooden
frames gives the building's modernist profile a
richly primitive and highly tactile quality.

Australian architect Sean Godsell has made it his ongoing mission to adapt the vernacular architecture of his native land to create a sustainable design philosophy suited for building in the twenty-first century. This has resulted in a portfolio of strikingly forward-looking projects that rely on a set of time-tested strategies for negotiating the extreme antipodean climate. For this three-bedroom weekend house, Godsell turned for inspiration to the breezeways and "sleep-outs" of the traditional outback homestead to create a structure that would endure the punishing summer sun as well as the gale-force winter winds whipping across the house's elevated beachfront site.

Though the initial impulse behind the design for this house may be rooted in the past, the house's form is evocative of some future time and place. Godsell raised the entire structure a full level off the ground and sheathed it in a protective skin of oxidized steel grating intended for industrial flooring. The grated skin is divided into panels that pivot open to act as a classic modernist *brise-soleil*, offering protection from the sun while allowing air to move through the house. When fully closed, the grated panels take on an armorlike aspect, giving the house an enigmatic, monolithic profile. Adding to the house's extraterrestrial quality is an entry stair suspended from the bottom of the structure like the gangway to a spaceship.

Inside, the house is organized into two main modules, one containing the main living space and kitchen, the other containing the three bedrooms and bathrooms as well as a study. Each of these two modules is accessed via external promenades, so that movement from the entry stair to the main living module and from the main living module to the bedrooms and bathrooms requires one to step outdoors. This circulation strategy evolved out of the client's request for a house that would put its inhabitants in touch with the elements and transport them away from the hermetically sealed, overly sanitized landscape of contemporary life.

Lower level

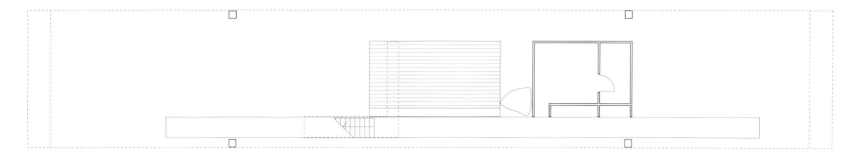

Upper level

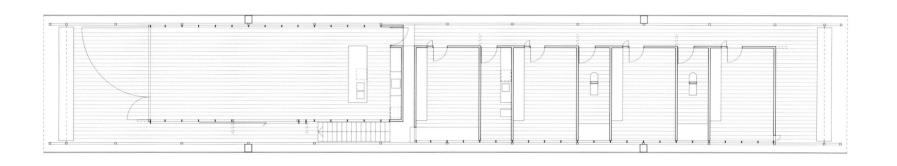

Roof

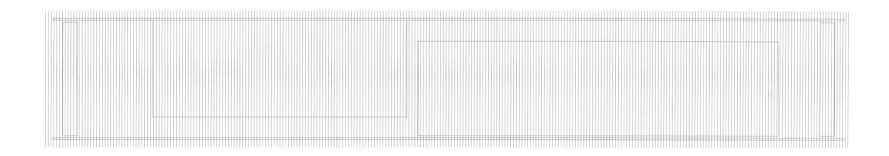

0	10	20	30 ft

Inspired by the traditional breezeways and "sleepouts" of the Australian outback, architect Sean Godsell raised the entire structure of the St. Andrews Beach House off the ground, with the resulting suspended gangway entry stair lending the already enigmatic house an extraterrestrial quality.

North elevation

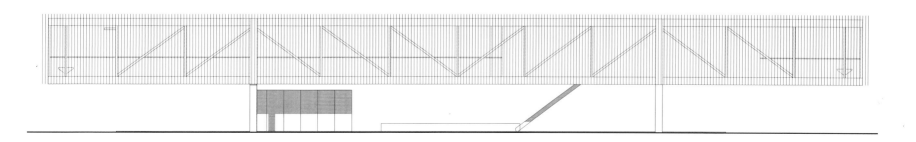

Above: The entry stair leads up to a series of spaces sheathed in a protective skin of oxidized steel grating intended for industrial flooring.

Opposite: The grated skin is divided into panels that pivot open to act as a classic modernist *brise-soleil*, offering protection from the sun while allowing air to move through the house.

Opposite: External promenades serve as corridors accessing the house's main living module and its sleeping module.

Above: The spare yet elegant bathrooms are organized around a slender, vertical mirrored panel.

Architects Felipe Assadi and Francisca Pulido let the natural drama of the Chilean landscape dictate the form for this modestly scaled weekend house. With a spectacular view of the mountains in the distance, the site for the Deck House brought to mind the form of a neatly inclined plane, inspiring the creation of a single planar terrace that unfolds from a swimming pool at the bottom of the site and up around the built volume of the house. The architects dedicated the greater part of the project's budget to the construction of the sculptural wooden deck form, letting the house proper occupy a simple rectangular volume open to breathtaking views of the surrounding mountains on all but one side.

The interior of the house is bifurcated by a wide wall that contains niches for the kitchen, storage space, and a fireplace facing the main living zone, which accommodates living and dining areas and the main sleeping area. On the other side of the dividing wall, dormitory-style sleeping berths are set within niches that occupy the long, narrow guest zone, with bathrooms and additional storage space efficiently placed at either end. When guests are not present, this dormitory section is easily closed off, leaving the main living zone as a simple glass pavilion open on three sides to the elegant contours of the wooden deck and the landscape gently sloping down to the neighboring valley.

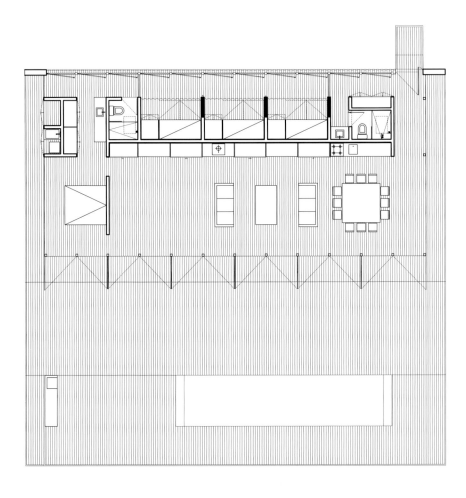

East elevation

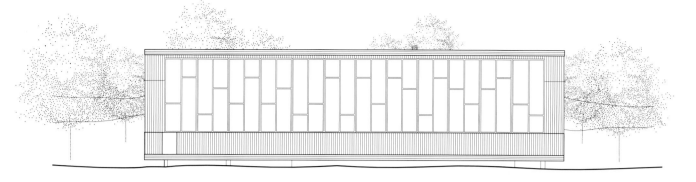

West elevation

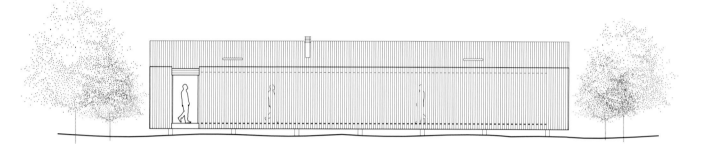

South elevation

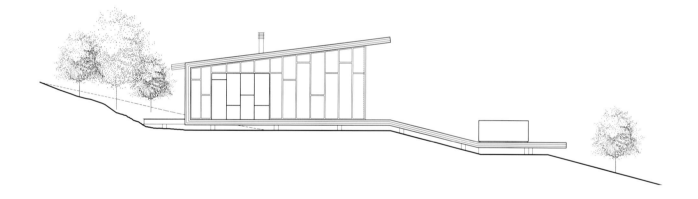

I	I	I
0	5	10 ft

Above: Architects Felipe Assadi and
Francisca Pulido conceived the Deck House
as a single planar terrace that unfurls
up from a swimming pool at the bottom
of the site and around the built volume of
the house.

Opposite: The main living zone
accommodates living and dining areas and
the main sleeping area, with a deep wall on
one side containing niches for the kitchen,
storage space, and a fireplace.

The house's exterior profile is a simple pavilion open on three sides to the elegant contours of the wooden deck and the landscape gently sloping down to the neighboring valley.

Located on Sydney's most northern peninsula, Peter Stutchbury and Phoebe Pape's Beach House was conceived to open up to its site on a sand dune. The architects arranged the house on two levels, with the first level largely devoted to an open-plan series of living spaces. With the exception of a hermetic guest suite at the front of the house, the ground level is a continuous promenade through a glazed entrance gallery to the kitchen and living and dining area, which can open completely on two sides via a system of retractable plate glass panels. A tatami area in one corner and a small, neatly orthogonal fish pond adjacent to the entrance gallery give a sense of intimacy, variety, and play to the sweeping space. Pape's role as an accomplished landscape designer deeply informs all of the firm's work, and the Beach House is no exception, as evidenced by the fluid relationship between the indoor space and the adjacent gardens, pond, and swimming pool.

Upstairs two bedrooms and a capacious master suite are organized along a single corridor. Whereas the ground level was conceived in a spirit of openness, the upper level is a series of closed spaces, sealed off even from the surrounding landscape, if desired, through an array of adjustable baffles. The architects have described the upper levels as a protective "canopy," a metaphor reinforced by the sweeping sculptural roof element, which also serves to conceal energy-conserving photovoltaic cells. Other strategies employed to maximize energy performance include the house's orientation on the site to benefit from prevailing winds, installation of a water heating and cooling system in the floor, and mist sprays at the pond and pool to optimize cooling.

Lower level

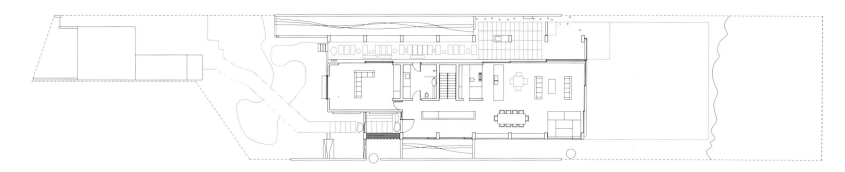

Upper level

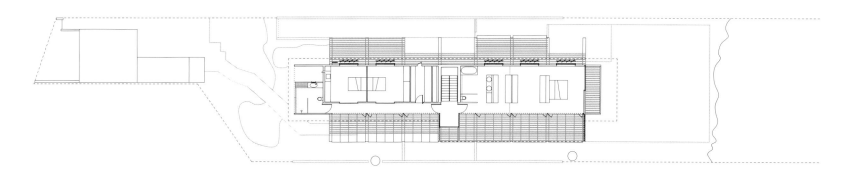

South elevation

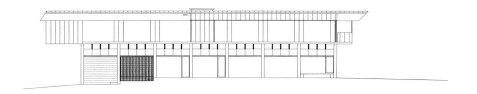

I   I   I
0   10   20 ft

Opposite: Peter Stutchbury and Phoebe Pape's Beach House is distinguished by a sweeping sculptural roof element that conceals energy-conserving photovoltaic cells.

Above: The main living and dining space can open completely on two sides via a system of retractable plate glass panels.

Pape's accomplishments as a landscape
designer informed the fluid relationship
between the indoor space and the adjacent
gardens, fishpond, and swimming pool.

All of the house's interior spaces, from
the expansive main living space to
the neatly organized bathrooms, employ
refined materials to achieve a high level
of finish.

Ben van Berkel and Caroline Bos, who founded UNStudio in 1999, exploded onto the American architectural scene with the inclusion of their Mobius House in the Museum of Modern Art's seminal exhibition "The Un-Private House." The ViLLA NM, a weekend house sited two hours north of Manhattan, is an American sequel of sorts for van Berkel and Bos. Where the Mobius House played with the idea of fitting all of the functions of domestic life into a looping structure, the ViLLA NM takes the classic modernist box and seems to begin to tear it into two volumes—one sloping downward, one thrusting up—creating a space-age version of the split-level tract house, with its slightly alien quality emphasized by the material palette of concrete, metal, and reflective glass.

This playfulness in the house's external form creates an internal organization arrayed around a series of walls that follows the arc created by the two bifurcated volumes, curving so that walls and floor are indistinguishable and forming a ramp-cum-passageway that unites the house's varying levels. The result is a spectacular architectural set piece that transforms the house's relatively modest program—living and dining spaces, kitchen, and three bedrooms—into a virtuoso riff on the modernist principle of the *promenade architecturale*. Sadly, this dazzling jewel of a house was destroyed by fire not long after its completion; the good news is that the clients intend to rebuild as soon as they are able.

First floor

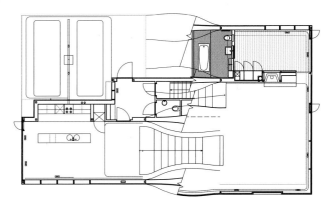

Second floor

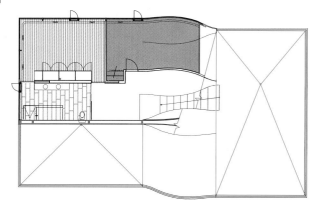

Cross sections

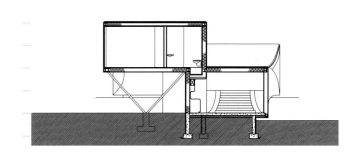

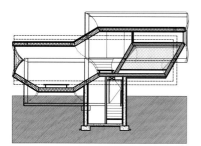

Longitudinal sections

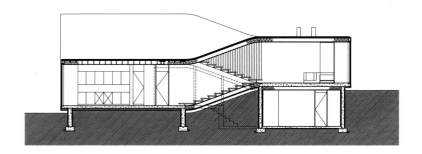

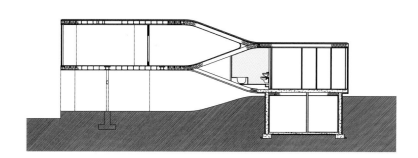

| | | |
0   10   20 ft

With VilLA NM, architects Ben van Berkel and Caroline Bos of UNStudio created a space-age version of the split-level tract house, with its slightly alien quality emphasized by the material palette of concrete, metal, and reflective glass.

Opposite: Inside, a series of walls that curve into the floor form a spectacular ramp-cum-passageway that unites the house's varying levels.

Above: The refined living room reflects the house's roots in the classic modernist box.

Whether experienced from inside the house
or on the highly reflective exterior glazing,
the formally ambitious structure's relationship
with the surrounding rural landscape is always
a harmonious one.

The international reputation of Werner Sobek has until recently rested largely on his impressive body of work as a structural engineer for large-scale projects around the globe, including Sony Plaza in Berlin and the Suvarnabhumi International Airport in Bangkok. However, in addition to being an engineer, Sobek is a trained architect who has taken on a second career as a designer of smaller-scale projects that push the cause of environmentally sustainable building strategies, beginning with a house he built for himself in 2000, which he dubbed R128. The house called H16, built outside of Stuttgart, Germany, further explores systems for sustainability; it is constructed from fully recyclable materials and capable of achieving zero net energy consumption and emissions.

As he did with R128, Sobek has given H16 an aesthetic profile that reflects the house's role as a machine for energy conservation. Materials for the two cubic volumes that compose the main part of the house are suitably lean and functional: The black base volume is built of prefabricated concrete panels and comprises the house's private zone, including three bedrooms, a study, and a particularly spacious master bathroom; the transparent upper volume, which accommodates an open living, kitchen, and dining area, is composed of triple-glazed panes treated to offer high thermal insulation. Both volumes are supported by a structural framework of recyclable steel that can be completely assembled or dismantled in a matter of days. A third, separate volume is connected to the main house by a steel terrace and contains the garage and service spaces.

In addition to the upper cube's highly insulated glass panes, which slide open to allow natural ventilation during temperate months, the house benefits from a geothermal heating and cooling system, as well as an array of photovoltaic panels that produces a surplus of energy, which is fed back to the public energy grid.

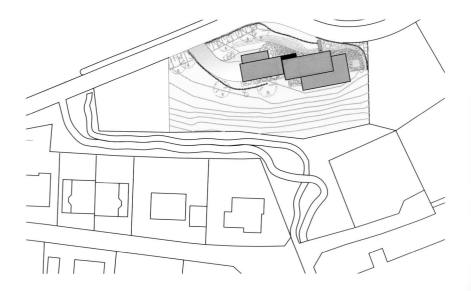

Lower level

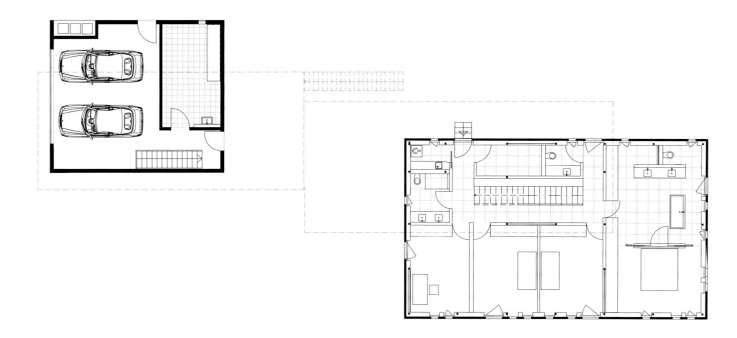

Upper level

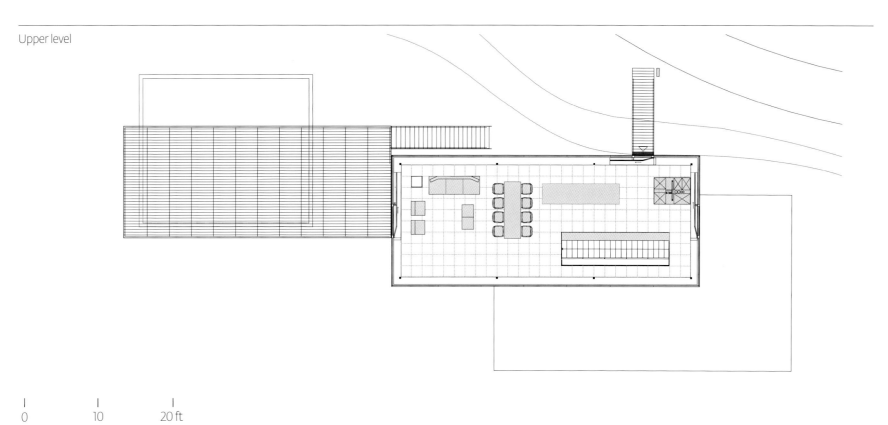

0   10   20 ft

Engineer and architect Werner Sobek's composition for H16 comprises two cubic volumes: The lower-level base volume contains the house's private zone; the transparent upper volume contains an open public zone.

Structural framework system

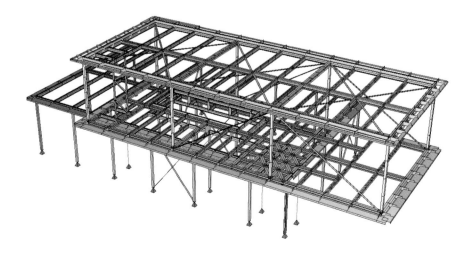

Above: Both volumes are supported by a
structural framework of recyclable steel,
visible on the house's upper level, that can
be completely assembled or dismantled
in a matter of days.

Opposite: The upper-level volume achieves
a maximum degree of transparency to take
advantage of views of the town and valley
at the foot of the site.

The lower and upper volumes are linked
by a stairway flanked by a bold red wall
outfitted with built-in shelves and cabinets.

Sir Christopher Wren's Christ Church Tower, dating from the latter half of the seventeenth century and reconstructed following damage during World War II, serves as the unlikely site for a dwelling extending over twelve levels, culminating in a 33-foot-tall volume that contains two mezzanines housing a library and viewing platform. The first three levels of the tower are composed of a living room, dining room, and mezzanine-level kitchen. The next five levels comprise a master bedroom and bathroom, a double-height space housing two additional bedrooms, and a floor dedicated to bathrooms and a utility room. In addition to three interior staircases, an elevator rises from the third to the ninth level.

In a task perhaps even more challenging than introducing these living spaces into the church tower, architects Nicholas Boyarsky and Nicola Murphy had to restore the structural fabric, which suffered from decades of neglect: The top half of the tower had long been exposed to the elements and retained little original interior material; the exterior Portland stone facade on the tower's lower half had suffered from atmospheric pollution, water damage, and infelicitous repairs. By focusing their efforts on retaining and repairing elements of the original design, such as the domical vault, the existing stairs (which now serve as a fire escape), and the vault at the upper levels, the architects managed to execute a serious structural renovation while creating an ambitious and whimsical series of spaces for contemporary living.

Sections

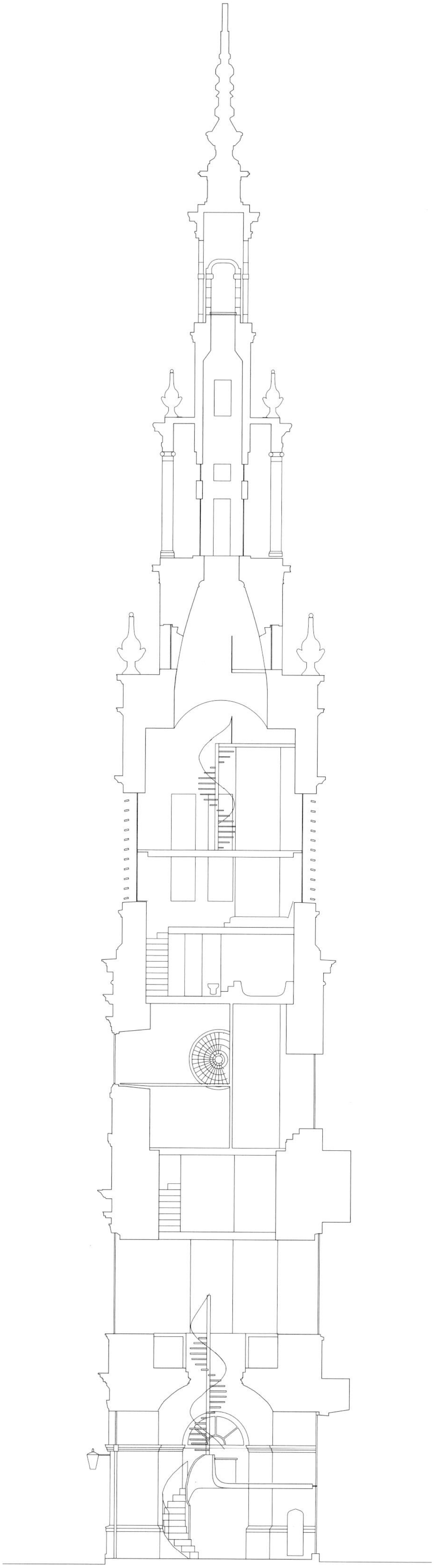

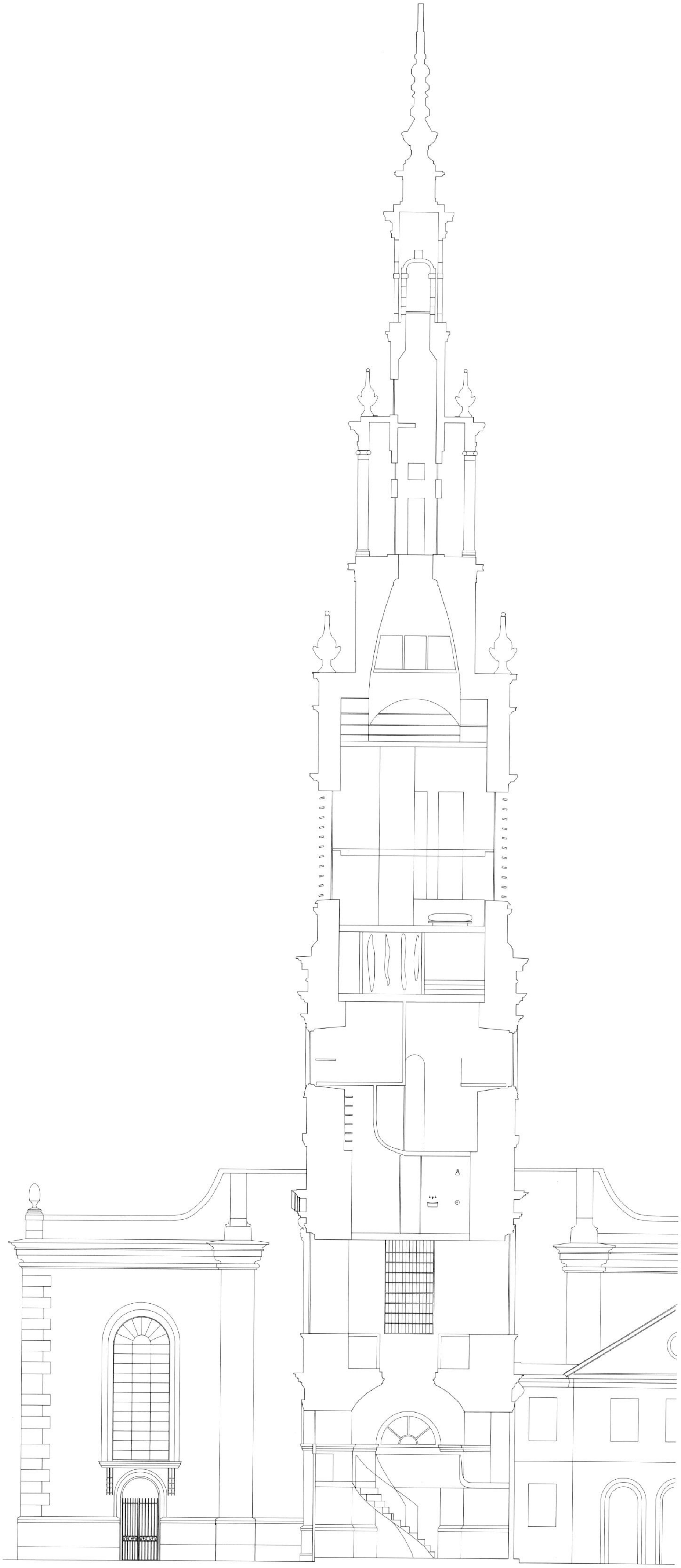

Level 1

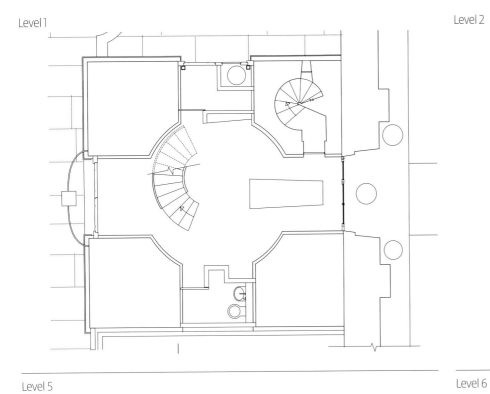

Level 2

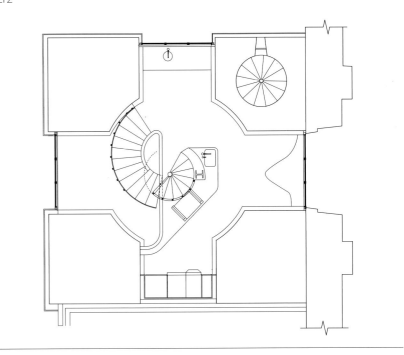

Level 5

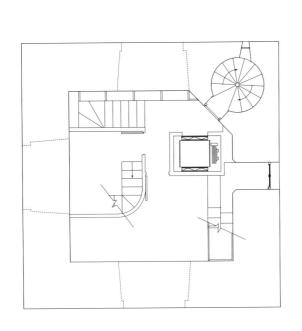

Level 6

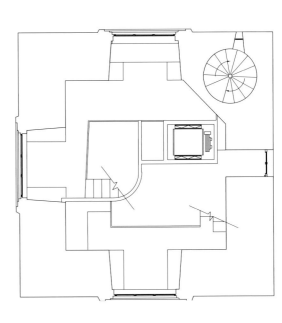

Level 9

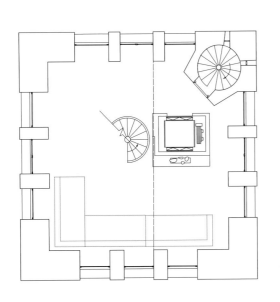

Level 10

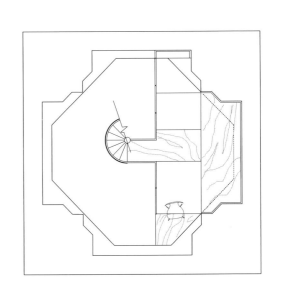

Level 3

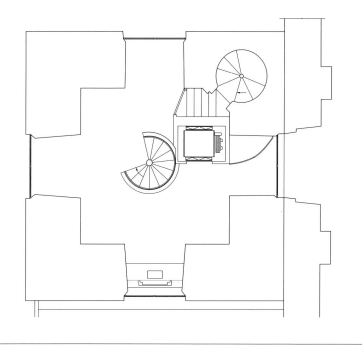

Level 4

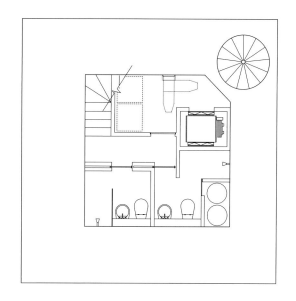

Level 7

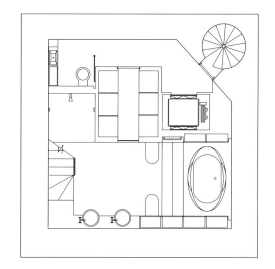

Level 8

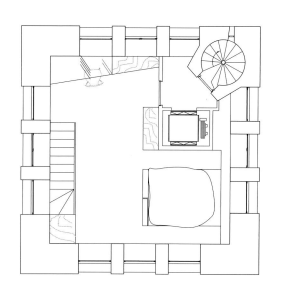

Level 11

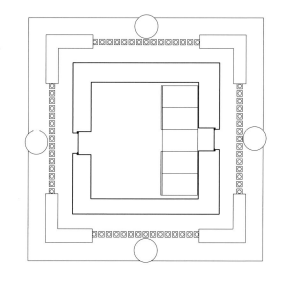

Level 12

0	5	10 ft

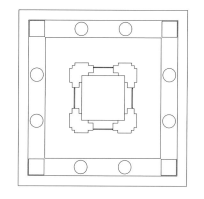

Boyarksy Murphy Architects completed a major
structural renovation introducing an ingenious
series of living spaces into Sir Christopher Wren's
Christ Church Tower, which dates from the
latter half of the seventeenth century.

Opposite: Because the dwelling extends over twelve levels, plus lofts and mezzanines, a dazzling variety of stairways are employed as well as an elevator between the third and ninth levels.

Above: All manner of niches and nooks within the original structure have been exploited to achieve the optimal use of the tower's irregular spaces.

Above: The tower's most generous spaces accommodate public-oriented rooms such as a salon on the ninth level and the foyer and dining room on the ground level.

Opposite: The kitchen is tucked beneath a dome and arranged around a spiral staircase.

Long before founding the firm MVRDV with Jacob van Rijs and Nathalie de Vries in 1991, Winy Maas had citymaking on his mind as an architect working in the office of Rem Koolhaas. Since then, MVRDV has realized the groundbreaking Dutch Pavilion for Expo 2000, the Silodam "megastructure" housing complex, and the master plan and architecture for The Hague's Ypenburg district, but Maas's most ingenious exercise in architecture and urbanism may be his addition to a loft atop a former garment factory in Rotterdam. Charged with accommodating a new master bedroom and two children's rooms, Maas introduced to the roof of the industrial building two separate structures, each taking the form of a child's vision of how a house should look. Around and between these houses Maas arranged two "plazas" connected by a "street," making the entire assemblage a sort of rooftop mini-city.

No less ingenious is what Maas accomplished inside. To optimize the privacy of each member of the family of four, Maas gave each of the three bedrooms its own spiral staircase leading up from the main living space on the top floor of the old loft building, with the two spiral staircases up to the children's semidetached rooftop rooms wrapping around each other in spectacular helical fashion. In line with the magical quality of the entire project, all of the pale wood staircases are suspended from the floor above so that they appear to hover over the floor of the original loft level.

Particular attention has been paid to the children's experience of the space, with a climbing rope leading up a tube at the center of their two intertwining spiral staircases and loft beds occupying two separate peaked roofs, where opened windows allow nighttime conversations between bedrooms. Outside, trees, tables, benches, and open-air showers create a parklike effect, while a coat of shocking blue polyurethane on every surface crowns the project with a playful LEGO quality.

Existing loft

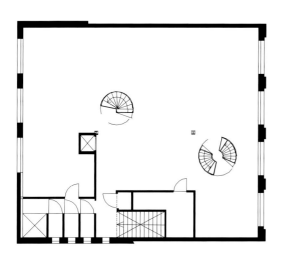

Addition

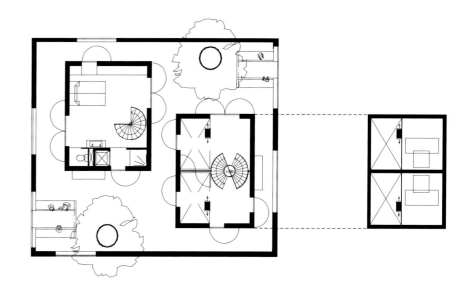

Roof

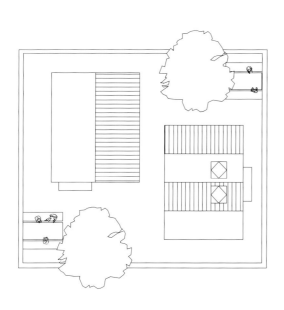

Cross section

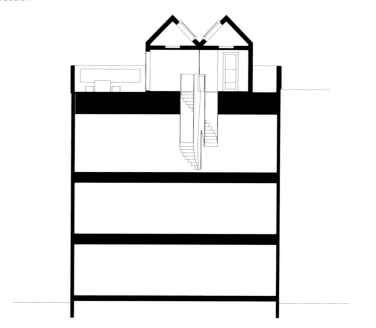

| | | |
|0| 10| 20 ft|

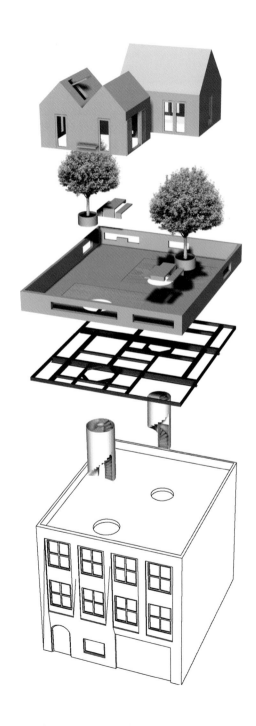

Above: Architect Winy Maas of MVRDV added three bedrooms in two separate "houses" to a loft in a former garment factory in Rotterdam.

Opposite: Between these two new structures Maas arranged two outdoor "plazas" connected by a "street," making the assemblage a rooftop mini-city.

Built-up diagram

Opposite: One of the new structures
is dedicated to a master bedroom and
bathroom, which has direct access to the
outdoor plaza as well as a private spiral
staircase leading down to the loft's main
living spaces.

Above: The two spiral staircases up to
the children's semidetached rooftop rooms
wrap around each other like a helix.

London-based architect David Adjaye has gained worldwide fame as a designer of spartan exhibition spaces, including the Rivington Place arts complex in London and the Museum of Contemporary Art in Denver, with a tendency to emphasize the sculptural possibilities inherent in the meticulous manipulation of natural light. In these sleek spaces a minimum of illumination goes a long way. His numerous house designs similarly rely on the formal qualities of light to create living spaces that favor a sense of compositional edginess over domestic comfort. With the Sunken House, commissioned by a fashion photographer friend, Adjaye found himself constructing a matte-black monolithic box among the Georgian brick town houses of East London's De Beavoir Town. Just as unconventional as the house's form was its method of construction, which Adjaye undertook in collaboration with a manufacturer of high-end prefabricated houses.

Composed of large prefabricated timber panels, the house's basic structure was assembled within a week. All the structural and exterior cladding panels, with windows and doorways cut out, were manufactured in Germany and delivered for assembly on site. For the exterior cladding Adjaye made the ingenious selection of the underside of thin-planked decking, which was then stained black. Inside spruce parapets and wainscoting relieve the stark white of the poured-resin floor in the main living space/photography studio, which crowns the house on its third story and is further distinguished by a 17-foot-long uninterrupted window span. The rest of the rooms are arranged on the house's lower two floors: master bedroom and study on the second floor; dining room and kitchen on the ground floor, partially excavated to access the sunken rear garden that gives the house its name.

North elevation

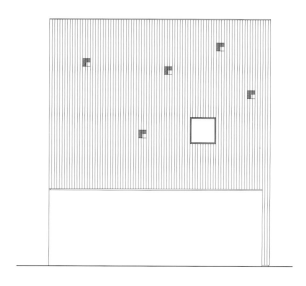

East elevation

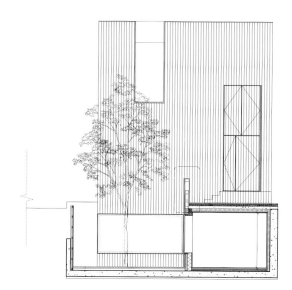

South elevation

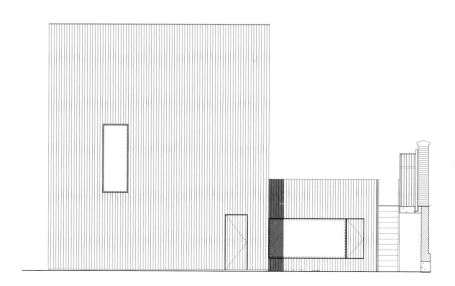

West elevation

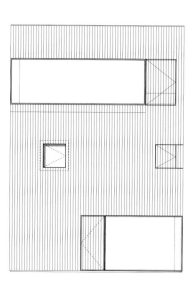

0	5	10 ft

Opposite: Architect David Adjaye designed the Sunken House as a matte-black monolithic box among the Georgian brick town houses of East London's De Beavoir Town.

Right: All the structural and exterior cladding panels, with windows and doorways cut out, were manufactured in Germany and delivered for assembly on site.

Section

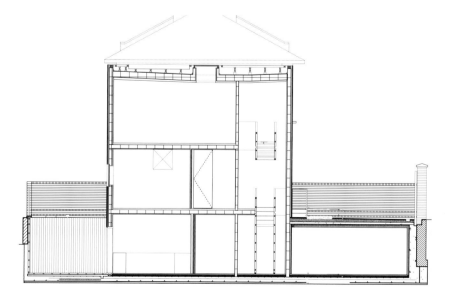

Opposite: The main living space/
photography studio, which crowns the
house on its third story, features a 17-foot-
long uninterrupted window span.

Above: One wall of the living space/
photography studio is composed of deep
blue cabinets concealing a hidden doorway,
at far right, leading to a small balcony.

Above: The warm wood in the kitchen and spruce parapets and wainscoting offer relief from the stark white of the plaster walls as well as the white poured-resin floor in the living space/photography studio.

Opposite: Fenestration was deliberately kept to a minimum to carefully frame views and provide dramatic natural illumination.

Though the site of the Wall House can accurately be described as suburban, its isolated and rustic conditions, placed in the shadow of the Andes Mountains, offer a rugged setting that is appropriate for this rough-hewn and formally playful dwelling. Instead of having one set of perimeter walls, as in a standard house, the Wall House has four sets of perimeter walls, each contributing different qualities of structure, function, and transparency.

Central to the house's spatial organization is a concrete core structure and ground-floor concrete slab, which accommodate gas-powered radiant heating as well as a PEX tubing system that keeps the house cool during warmer months. Together these strategies compose a climate-control system that is far more efficient than standard HVAC systems. Living areas—kitchen, dining area, and guest room—arrayed around the concrete core comprise the second layer of spatial delimitation, with custom wood shelving serving as an independent, more permeable interior wall system.

The third layer is composed of what architects Marc Frohn and Mario Rojas Toledo describe as a "milky shell," a system of high-insulation polycarbonate panels that encloses two double-height spaces containing the living room and the master bedroom, respectively. These translucent panels function in tandem with the house's final layer of enclosure, a soft fabric membrane typically used in the construction of greenhouses; while air in the translucent polycarbonate panels provides insulation, the fabric membrane further shields the house from heat gain by reflecting 70 percent of its UV intake. The spaces created beneath this membrane function as a tentlike porch that can be opened or closed, and the alternating folding and translucent surfaces on the house's exterior give the entire structure a cut-diamond profile evocative of its spectacular mountain setting.

Wall House Santiago, Chile FAR frohn&rojas 2007

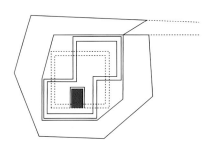
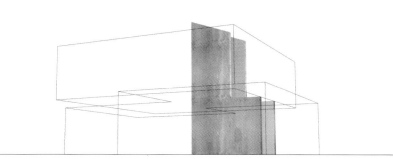

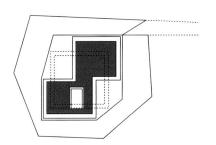

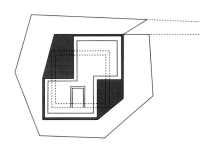
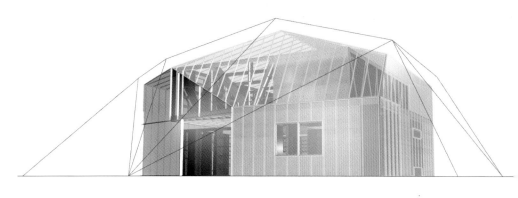

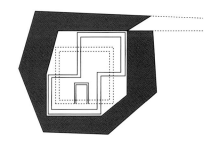
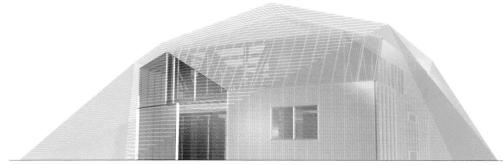

Upper level

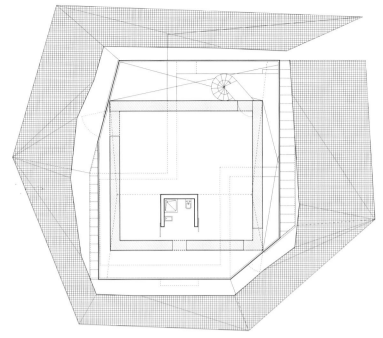

Lower level

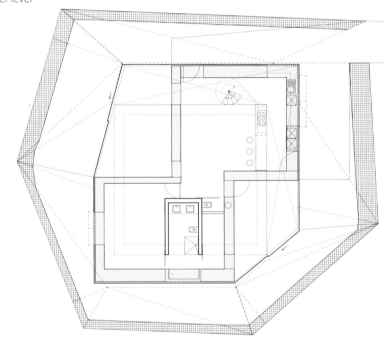

Section

0	10	20 ft

Architects FAR frohn&rojas composed the Wall House of four sets of perimeter walls, each contributing different qualities of structure, function, and transparency.

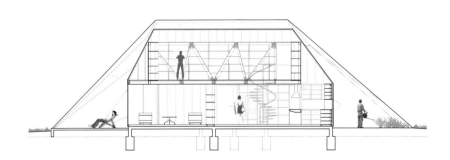

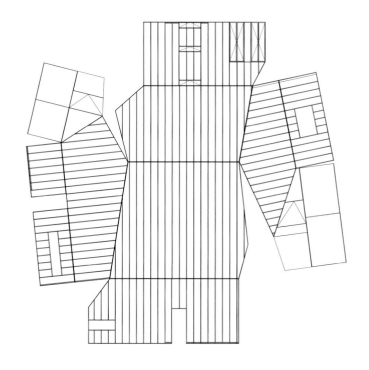

The house's outermost "wall" is a soft fabric membrane typically used in the construction of greenhouses; the spaces created beneath this membrane function as a tentlike porch that can be opened or closed.

Unfolded exterior surfaces

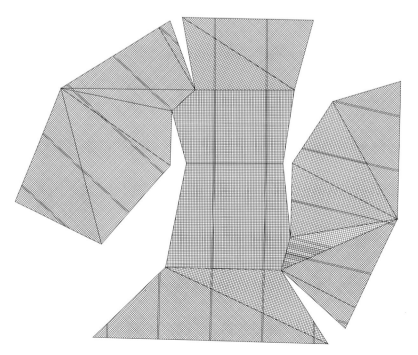

Interior spaces are enclosed by what the architects describe as a "milky shell" of high-insulation polycarbonate panels, while custom wood shelving serves as a more permeable interior wall system.

Unfolded upper- and lower-floor shelves

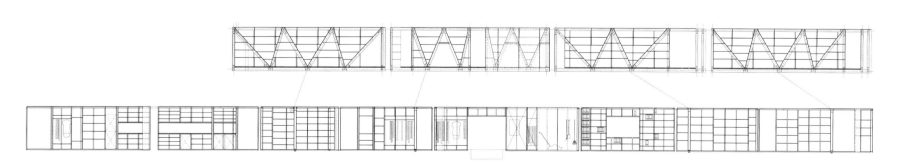

Above and opposite, top: A concrete core structure and ground-floor concrete slab comprise the house's innermost structural layer.

Opposite, bottom: Throughout the house the architects employed low-cost materials such as unfinished concrete and plywood panels and doors.

With a few simple but remarkably bold gestures, architect Sou Fujimoto has created a transfixing weekend house on the rocky Pacific coastline outside of Chiba, two hours' drive from Tokyo. From the approach to its entrance, the house appears as an assemblage of solid concrete cubes, more sculptural form than habitable space. Once inside, the agglomeration of cubes reveals itself to be a continuous 10-foot-wide network of branching corridorlike spaces that effectively form one continuous room. Adding to the singular character of this residence is the near absolute openness on its seaside facade, where floor-to-ceiling plate glass walls offer a striking contrast to the blank solidity of the house's entry facade.

Living room, dining area, kitchen, study, master bathroom, and traditional tatami room unfold along the branching plan, which the architect has likened to a trail on the coastline, where each room is a comfortable space discovered along the way. In this sense, Fujimoto fulfilled his intention to design a house that was essentially primitive or, as he puts it, "in between natural and manmade." This organic layout also allows the different rooms to assume a variety of orientations toward the ocean, creating a multiplicity of views. But just as the entry and oceanfront facades of the house offer an object lesson in contrast, so does the highly refined execution of the interior concrete work and frameless glazed walls oppose the primitivist impulse at the heart of this small but ambitious project.

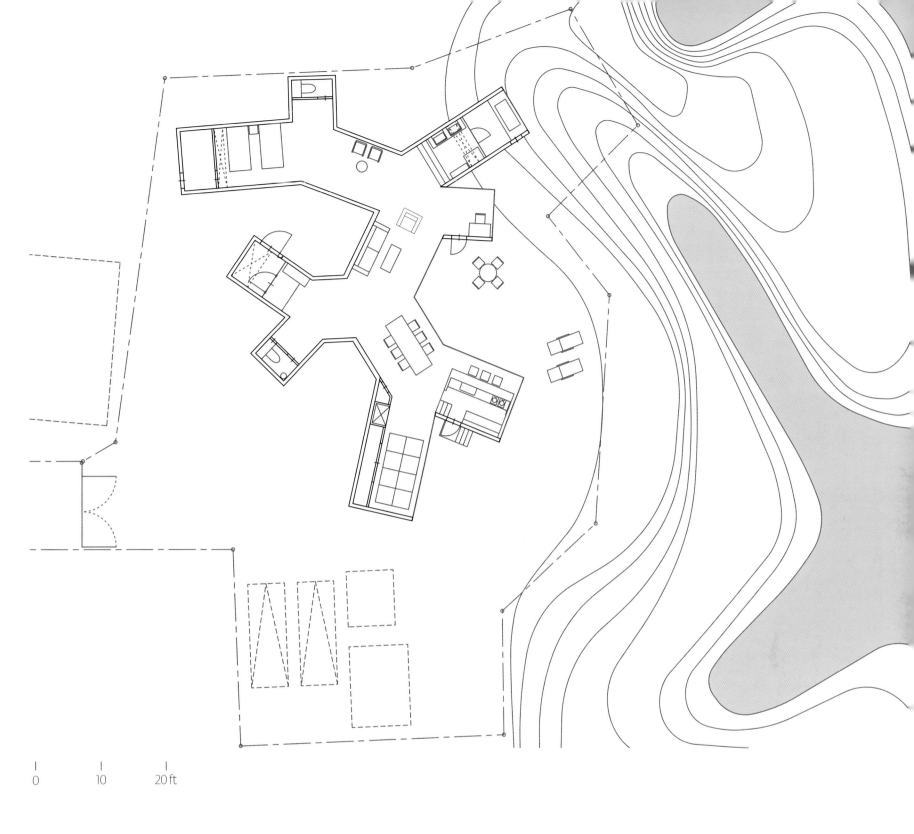

I   I   I
0   10   20 ft

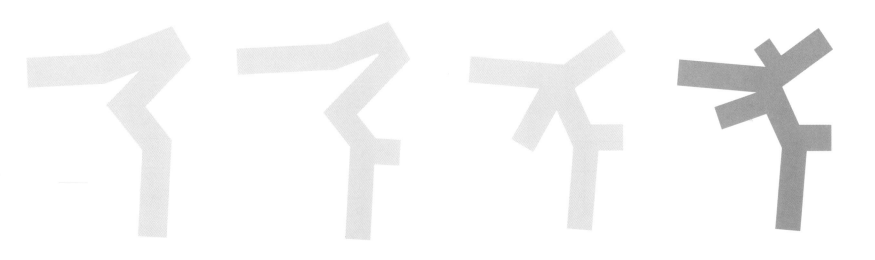

The branching, organic organization of
Sou Fujimoto's House O appears as an
assemblage of solid concrete cubes on its entry
facade, while its seaside facade is composed
entirely of floor-to-ceiling plate glass walls.

Plan evolution diagram

Opposite, clockwise from top left:
Dining room and kitchen; living room;
bedroom; study.

Above: Fujimoto conceived the house's
interior as a trail on the coastline, where
each room is a comfortable space
discovered along the way.

When a prominent Swiss art dealer approached Andreas Fuhrimann and Gabrielle Hächler to build a vacation home in the remote village of Vnà, the architects immediately were enticed by the challenge of introducing a modern form into a firmly traditional context. The tiny village in Switzerland's Engadine Valley boasts a population of only seventy residents and a largely unaltered built landscape, rooted in a centuries-old regional style that the architects wanted to approximate without lapsing into historicist pastiche.

The choice of lightweight concrete as the house's primary building material was determined by the stone construction characteristic of the region; the massive perforated wooden front door is also a nod to local building traditions. The overall structure of the house is composed of three floors, the first of which is largely devoted to an open multipurpose room intended as a space for exhibitions and entertaining. The second floor accommodates three bedrooms, and the top level contains the kitchen and the main living and dining space, which enjoys the house's most generous views of the surrounding mountain landscape through an outsize oriel window. The concrete kitchen and fireplace provide structural support for the top floor's sculptural gabled ceiling, which, along with the walls of the living space and bedrooms, is clad in plywood paneling to create a decidedly contemporary version of a warm, protective mountainside shelter.

Rather than imposing a conventionally modernist grid dictating the placement of windows and structural details on the house's facade, the architects chose to let the arrangement of the interior spaces determine the arrangement of exterior form, giving the elevations an informal, colloquial quality. Also softening the austerity of the architects' overarching modernist approach to the project are the deep asymmetrical reveals along the edges of the windows. In addition, the large oriel windows on the top two floors project idiosyncratically, and a sculptural, nonorthogonal treatment of surfaces extends to the interior walls as well, so that every surface, detail, and structural element negotiates the distance between the rural mountainside vernacular of the Engadine Valley and the high modernist style of the early twenty-first century.

First floor

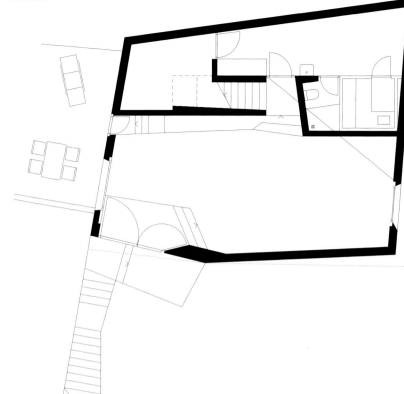

Second floor

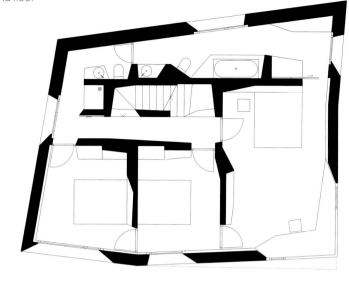

Third floor

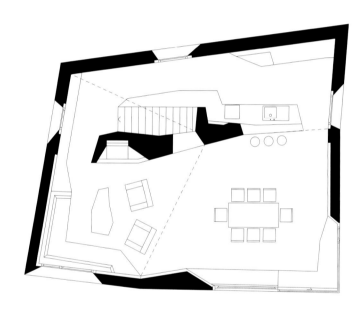

```
|         |         |         |
0        10        20 ft
```

North elevation

East elevation

South elevation

West elevation

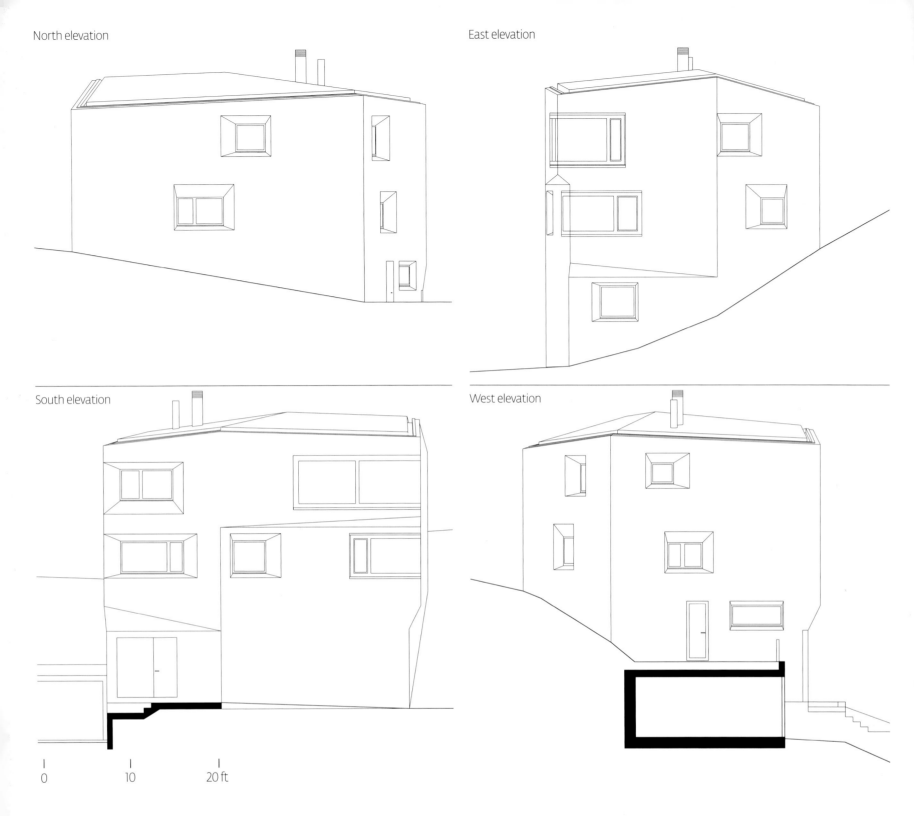

0   10   20 ft

Above left: Architects Andreas Fuhrimann and Gabrielle Hächler strove to refer to local building traditions in the design of the Presenhuber House, demonstrated by the massive perforated wooden front door.

Above right and opposite: The architects softened their modernist approach with such details as windows with deep asymmetrical reveals and idiosyncratic corner oriels.

Opposite and above left: The concrete kitchen and fireplace provide structural support for the top floor's sculptural gabled ceiling.

Above right: The bedrooms as well as the living space are clad in plywood paneling, giving the rooms a particularly contemporary warmth.

Opposite: The main living space on the house's top level enjoys the most generous views of the surrounding mountain landscape through an outsize oriel window.

Above: The entry level is largely devoted to an open multipurpose room intended as a space for exhibitions and entertaining.

The young family who commissioned this project wanted a house with loosely arranged, open spaces that would provide an overall atmosphere of connectedness, while accommodating discrete spaces that would allow a reasonable degree of privacy. To achieve this, architects Tobias Kraus and Timm Schönberg conceived the house as a partially excavated, glass-enclosed indoor "terrace" that contains an expansive living/dining/kitchen space and serves as the platform for an elevated sequence of individual rooms arranged in a complex series of slightly varying levels. The open public zone on the lower floor and the three bedrooms in the upper-level private zone are united by a spectacular central atrium-cum-library, around which all other interior spaces are organized, and which features a continuous bookshelf that ascends the more than two-story height of the house.

Both the openness of the ground floor and the secluded nature of the upper level are carefully modulated. Though enclosed by large-plate clear glazing, the main living spaces on the ground floor also feel protected by the concrete parapet of the ground floor's partial excavation out of the sloping site. The arrangement of the small, numerous upper-level rooms on linked platforms of varying heights gives this area an intentionally warrenlike quality, but each space is punctuated by apertures overlooking both the exterior garden and the interior atrium, so that there is an ever-present sense of permeability. The varying levels of the upper floor result in a ceiling of fluctuating heights on the ground floor, lending complexity to the otherwise simple open plan of the main living spaces.

The sophisticated spatial organization of the house is achieved within a notably cost-effective structure: Digitally measured and cut, mass-produced wood panels comprise all the walls and floors on the house's upper level. A similarly economical approach was given to the house's energy use, with geothermal power responsible for heating.

Lower level

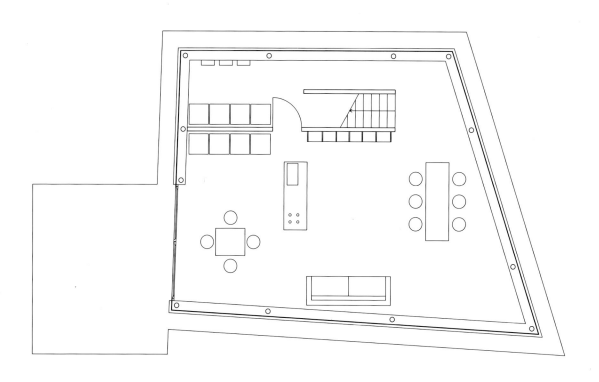

Upper level

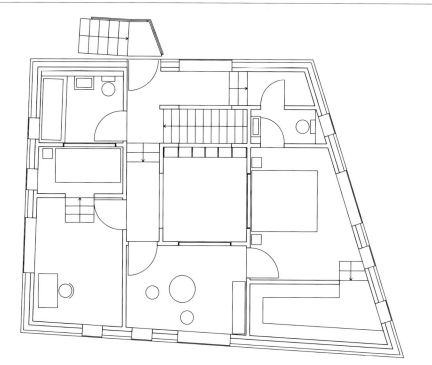

0   10   20 ft

North elevation

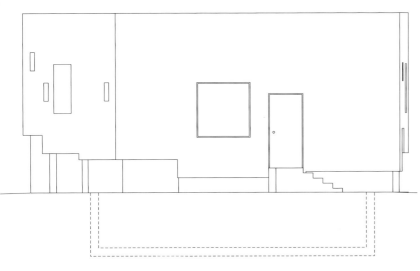

West elevation

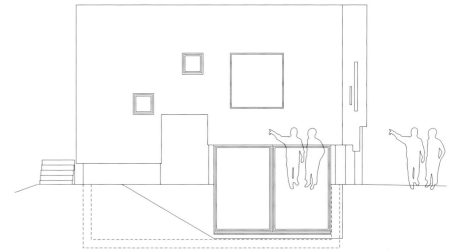

South elevation

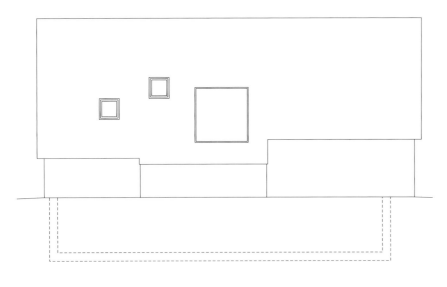

East elevation

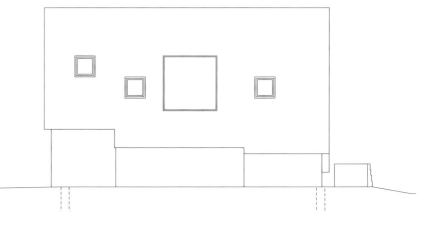

0	10	20 ft

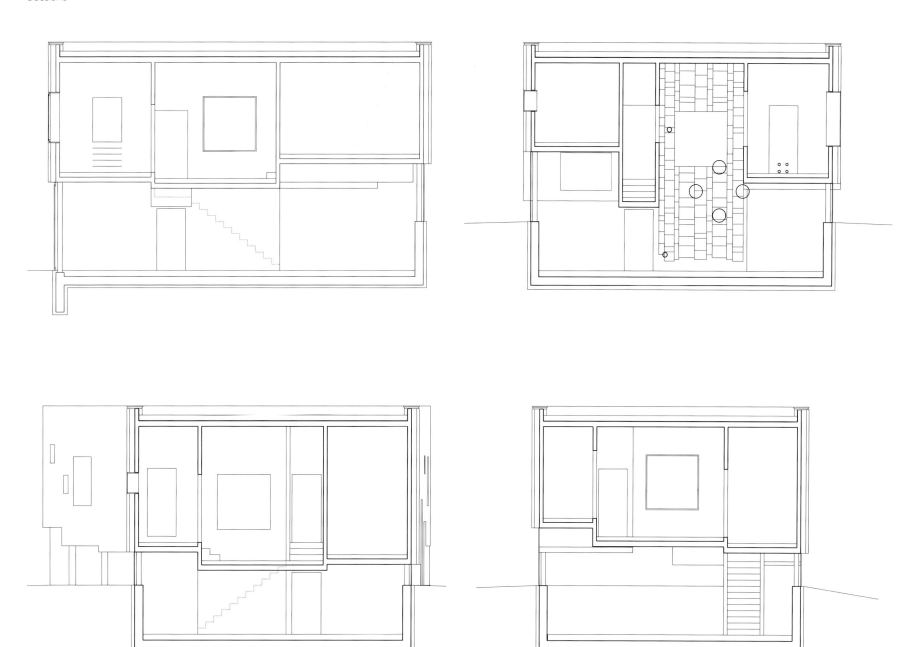

Kraus Schönberg Architects conceived the house as a glass-enclosed indoor "terrace" protected by the concrete parapet of the ground floor's partial excavation out of the sloping site.

The open public zone on the lower level and the three bedrooms in the upper-level private zone are united by a spectacular central atrium-cum-library, which features a continuous bookshelf that ascends the more than two-story height of the house.

The upper-level rooms are punctuated by apertures overlooking both the exterior garden and the interior atrium, giving an ever-present sense of permeability.

In designing a vacation house for a young family that intended to use it year-round, architects Tim Hay and Jeff Fearon turned for inspiration to the tradition of rugged, simple construction that characterizes New Zealand's Southern Lakes region, where the project is located. The architects envisioned modestly scaled spaces, sufficiently flexible and durable to accommodate a generous number of guests during even the most intemperate conditions on a rocky, densely forested site. This vision came to fruition in the form of a compact two-bedroom cabin clad in heavy stone and partially tucked into the slope of its mountaintop site.

The insertion of the house into the hillside creates an entry sequence that begins at the roof, where a deck, a small metal chimney pipe, and a delicate railing are all that is visible of the house. A narrow staircase slicing through the deck leads down to the floor-to-ceiling sliding glass wall of the open-plan main living space, where kitchen, dining, and living areas enjoy panoramic views from the fully glazed, cantilevered corner, made even more dramatic by the placement of a podlike suspended fireplace. Adjacent to this is the master bedroom, which can be fully opened or closed off from the living space, depending on the degree of privacy required. A surprisingly generous space for bathing, considering the overall dimensions of the house, links the master bedroom to a smaller bunkroom that can accommodate up to two families.

Sandblasted concrete floors and walls accented by rich cedar boards, blackened steel framework, and a polished plaster ceiling create a sense at once of luxury and durability. The insulated glazing and heavyweight stone construction provide significant passive protection from extreme high and low temperatures in the region during summers and winters, with radiant heating from the insulated floor slab available during the most difficult winter conditions. The project's frontier roots are evidenced by its relative self-sufficiency: Though the house receives electricity service, it also depends on its own bottled gas source and relies entirely on an adjacent mountain stream for its water, which is stored in a tank and UV-filtered.

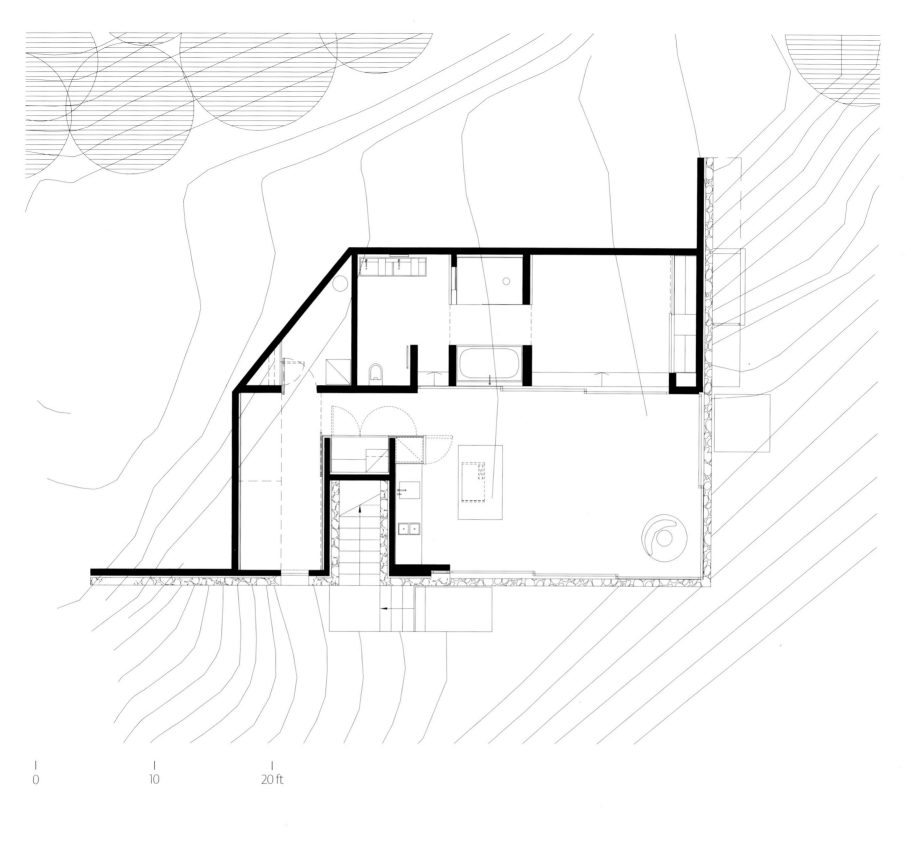

Opposite: The compact two-bedroom cabin designed by Fearon Hay Architects is clad in heavy stone and partially tucked into the slope of its mountaintop site.

Right: Two sides of the cabin open to the surrounding landscape via sliding floor-to-ceiling glass panes.

Section

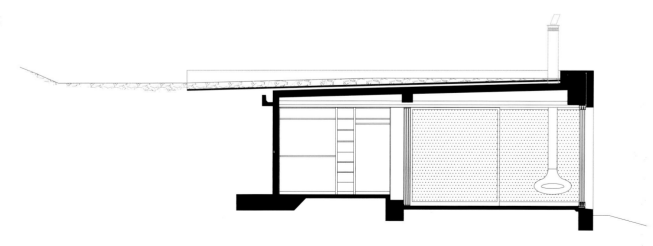

Above: Sandblasted concrete floors and walls accented by rich cedar boards, blackened steel framework, and a polished plaster ceiling create a sense of luxury that belies the cabin's modest scale.

Opposite: The kitchen, dining, and living areas enjoy panoramic views from the fully glazed, cantilevered corner, made even more dramatic by the placement of a podlike suspended fireplace.

Sections

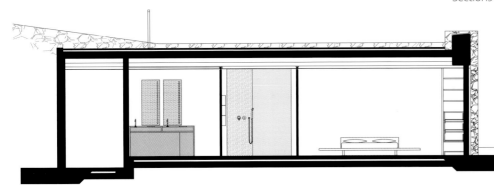

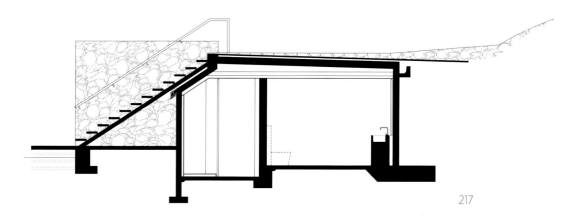

Set on a forested hillside site overlooking the Hudson River, across from West Point, the Olnick Spanu House appears as a miragelike, light-as-air, pristine pavilion in the wilderness thanks to architect Alberto Campo Baeza's strategy of creating an elegant structure that would not impose itself onto the spectacular rustic landscape but rather would, to use the architect's term, "underline" it. Campo Baeza—who has earned international acclaim for numerous houses completed in his native Spain and for whom this house is his first project to be completed in the United States—took a literal approach to the concept of underlining, conceiving of a form for the house that would seem to be composed of only a few decisive horizontal lines echoing the strong horizontals of the river bank below and the tree line above.

To achieve this effect of ephemeral horizontality Campo Baeza placed a 94-foot-long by 25-foot-wide glass pavilion on a 112-foot-long by 54-foot-wide concrete box that is tucked into the slope of the site. This discreetly enclosed lower floor accommodates bedrooms and extensive mechanical and services spaces as well as a spacious central hall that functions as a gallery for the clients' collection of Arte Povera and contemporary Italian art. The glass pavilion on the upper floor, which also functions as a showcase for the clients' collection, is an open space comprising living area, dining area, library, and kitchen with space for informal dining. Two freestanding white volumes—each containing stairs and, respectively, an elevator plus a niche for one of the kitchen's countertops and a powder room—break up the glass-enclosed expanse of the upper floor. Outside, the pavilion opens onto the roof of the concrete plinth, which has been surfaced in elegant travertine stone. The glass pavilion is capped with a substantial overhanging flat white roof that cantilevers as much as 10 feet over the travertine terrace on the house's river-facing side, providing a nicely sheltered outdoor space and further emphasizing the planar horizontality underlying the house's composition.

Lower level

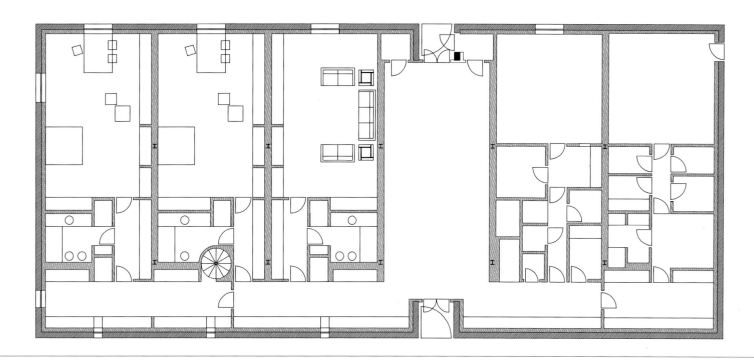

Upper level

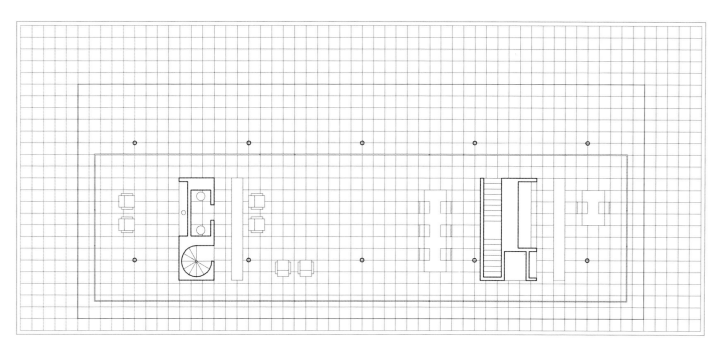

| | | |
0 2   10 ft

On a forested site overlooking the Hudson River
architect Alberto Campo Baeza created an
elegant structure that "underlines" the landscape
rather than imposing itself upon it.

Campo Baeza's strong yet simple concept for the house is composed of a light glass pavilion placed on a concrete box that is tucked into the slope of the site.

Opposite: The house's lower level serves as a concrete plinth, which has been surfaced in elegant travertine stone to serve as a terrace onto which the upper-level pavilion opens on all sides.

Above: The glass pavilion on the upper floor is an open space comprising living area, dining area, library, and kitchen with space for informal dining.

Above: The library offers a more intimately
scaled interior space within the glass pavilion.

Opposite: The house's overhanging flat
white roof cantilevers 10 feet over
the travertine terrace on the house's
river-facing side, providing a nicely sheltered
outdoor space.

This small but monumental house, located in a coastal resort region in the southeast of Japan, was born out of an intense yet remarkably harmonious collaboration between the architects and client. Tokyo-based architects Takaharu and Yui Tezuka received the commission from a fine arts academic who had recently retired from organizing large-scale contemporary art installations. The client's highly refined sense of form and space informed the Tezukas' approach to the project at every level, from the determination that wall space be maximized in order to accommodate a large art collection to the placement of the bathroom sink within a niche, leaving unobstructed the view out from the bathtub.

Taking advantage of the site's panoramic view of Ushimado Bay, the architects arranged all of the living spaces—main living and dining area, efficient galley kitchen, bathroom, one large bedroom, plus a small garage—along a single axis, like a railcar. The side of the house facing away from the bay is opaque except for a continuous band of clerestory windows, while the side of the house overlooking the bay can be entirely open via a system of retractable sliding doors, which effectively eliminate one entire perimeter wall from the house. Even with the sliding panels open, however, the house enjoys a sense of enclosure thanks to the high solid wall that reaches up to the double-height ceiling, seeming to hover above the long aperture, which opens to a view framed by a deep, shade-giving overhang. This high ceiling also creates a dramatic sense of proportion, particularly within the house's smaller spaces, where the lofty ceiling height becomes thrillingly exaggerated. The spare, ethereal quality of the expanses of plaster inside the house is nicely countered by exterior siding of charred Japanese cedar, a traditional building material for which the region is famed.

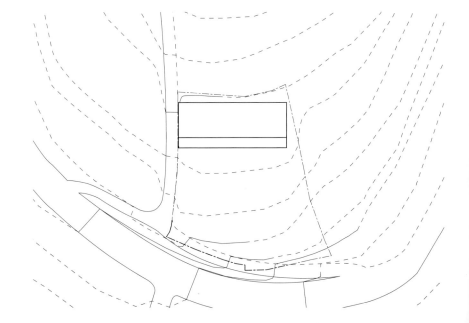

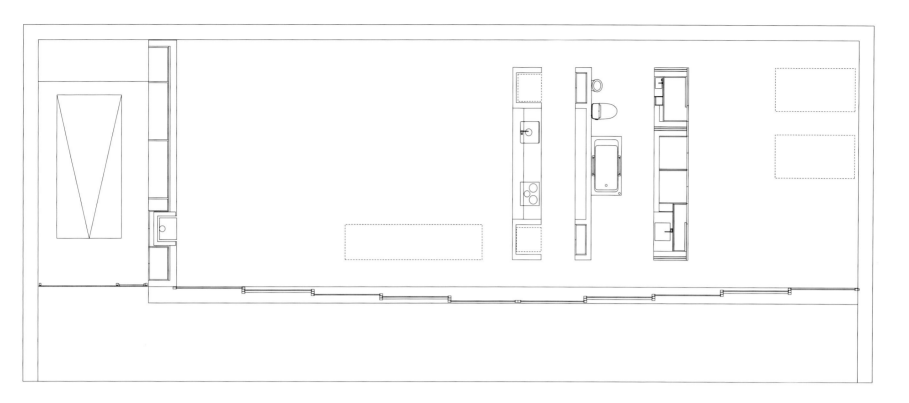

0   10   20 ft

Opposite: The small yet monumental Atelier in Ushimado is the elegant product of an intense collaboration between Tezuka Architects and their client, a fine arts academic.

Right: The house can be entirely open on one side via a system of retractable sliding doors that effectively eliminate one entire perimeter wall from the house.

Cross section

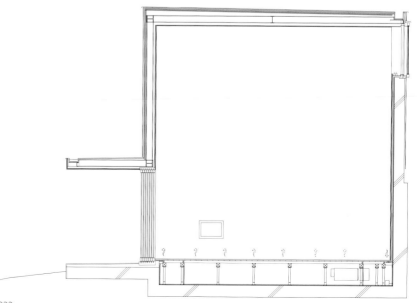

The main living area was designed
to provide maximum wall space to
accommodate a large art collection.

236

Bedroom, bathroom, and kitchen are arranged in linear sequence along a single axis like a railcar.

At the edge of London's fabled Highgate Cemetery stands a crystalline composition in glass and concrete that offers a surprisingly harmonious counterpoint to the Victorian funereal monuments and High-Gothic overgrowth of vegetation that the house surveys. Architects Nick Eldridge and Piers Smerin were charged with building a new structure on the site of an existing house by respected British modernist John Winter on a remote perimeter of the cemetery, which is something of a tourist attraction thanks largely to the presence of Karl Marx's grave. However, since the house's situation in the cemetery's northeast corner is mostly undisturbed by visitors, the architects felt free to open the south and west facades of the house, which occupies the footprint of the original Winter house, to the moody views of the cemetery, an adjacent park, and the London skyline in the distance.

The architects arranged the house's interior spaces among four floors, including a basement level. Each of the three main living levels accommodates a generously proportioned bedroom with a terrace, and the main living space is completely exposed on two sides. In an inversion of conventional residential layouts, the expansive kitchen and dining space occupy the topmost level of the house, along with a study. Here a spectacular retractable glass roof over the entire kitchen opens the already highly transparent space to the elements in supremely dramatic fashion. The overall sense of transparency is maximized by the study's frameless glass work surface running along one of the floor-to-ceiling glass walls, creating a shimmering, pristine workspace virtually thrust into the sublime disarray of the nineteenth-century cemetery.

Basement

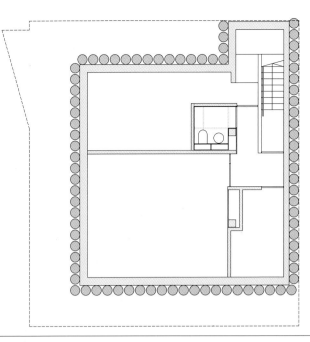

First floor

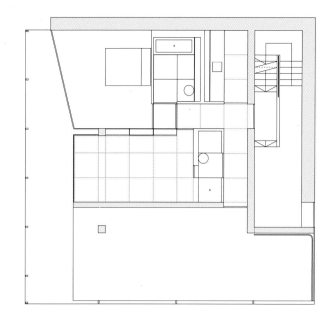

Second floor

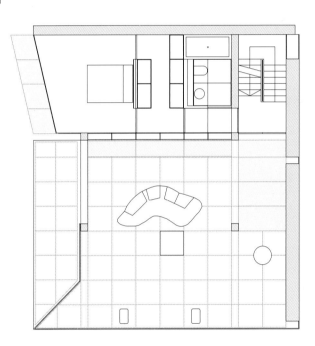

Third floor

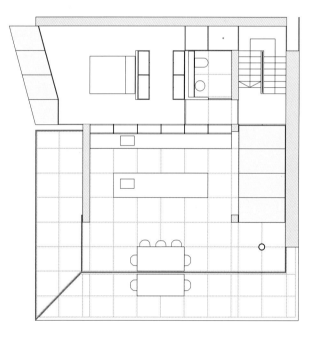

0   10   20 ft

Opposite: Architects Eldridge Smerin
created a glass and concrete structure that
is surprisingly harmonious with the adjacent
Victorian cemetery.

Right: The house's street facade of black
granite, translucent glass, and black steel panels
presents a highly opaque contrast to the
facades facing the cemetery.

East elevation

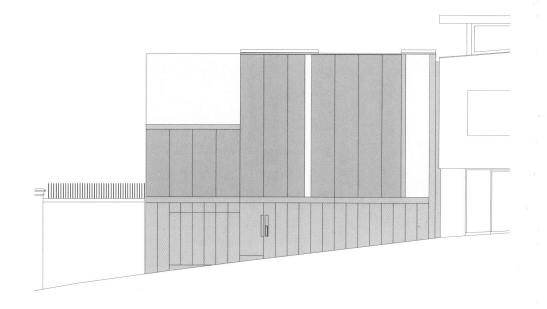

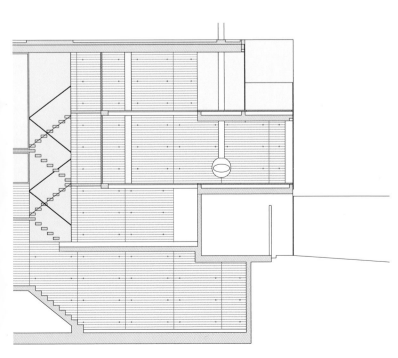

Opposite, left: In addition to large expanses of floor-to-ceiling glass, the cemetery-facing facades enjoy generous terraces.

Opposite, right: The house's interior concrete walls, particularly in the stairwell, maintain a strong horizontal pattern from the timber boards used to shutter the concrete.

Above left: The complete glazing of the house's south and west facades provides spectacular vistas over the cemetery.

Above right: Transparent glass floor panels on the house's top two floors permit natural light down to the entry hall.

Section

Above: The study's frameless glass work surface is virtually thrust into the cemetery.

Opposite: Black granite floors, built-in cabinetry of reflective black lacquer, and exposed concrete ceilings give the main living space a hard-edged quality that unexpectedly complements the lush, moody landscape outside.

In the kitchen, a retractable glass roof opens the already highly transparent space to the elements in dramatic fashion.

Sacred
to the Memory of
SUSANNAH FOXWELL.
DIED APRIL 28TH 1849.
AGED 23 YEARS.
SUSANNAH GRACE FOXWELL
DIED MAY 7TH 1852.
AGED 3 YEARS.

Split House
Asakawa Satoshi: pp. 12–13, 15
Fu Xing: p. 14

4 x 4 House
Courtesy Tadao Ando Architect &
Associates

House in Manhattan
Christian Richters

Casa BR
Nelson Kon

Casa Tóló
Fernando Guerra: pp. 50–51
Duccio Malagamba: pp. 46–49, 52–55

Casa Poli
Cristobal Palma

Brick House
Hélène Binet

St. Andrews Beach House
Earl Carter

Turbulence House
Paul Warchol

Deck House
Cristobal Palma

Ten Broeck Cottage
Elizabeth Felicella: pp. 74, 77 bottom,
    79 right
Tom McWilliam: pp. 75, 76, 77 top, 78,
    79 left

Beach House
Michael Nicholson

VilLA NM
Christian Richters

Sunken House
Ed Reeve

H16
Zooey Braun

Wall House
Cristobal Palma

Christ Church Tower
Hélène Binet

House O
Edmund Sumner/VIEW

Didden Village
Robert Hart

Presenhuber House
Valentin Jeck

Acknowledgments

Thank you to the architects and photographers whose brilliant work fills these pages. I am also grateful to Abrams editor in chief Eric Himmel and publisher Steve Tager for their enthusiastic support, and to editor Aiah Wieder for patiently guiding this publication to completion. Special thanks go to graphic designer Beatriz Cifuentes-Caballero for her elegant and intelligent work.